Life Skills for Teens

Level Up Your Confidence, Social Skills, and Time & Money Smarts To Own Your Future

Celeste Avonly

Copyright © 2024 by Celeste Avonly

All rights reserved.

No portion of this book may be reproduced in any form without written permission from the publisher or author, except as permitted by U.S. copyright law.

This publication is designed to provide accurate and authoritative information in regard to the subject matter covered. It is sold with the understanding that neither the author nor the publisher is engaged in rendering legal, investment, accounting or other professional services. While the publisher and author have used their best efforts in preparing this book, they make no representations or warranties with respect to the accuracy or completeness of the contents of this book and specifically disclaim any implied warranties of merchantability or fitness for a particular purpose. No warranty may be created or extended by sales representatives or written sales materials. The advice and strategies contained herein may not be suitable for your situation. You should consult with a professional when appropriate. Neither the publisher nor the author shall be liable for any loss of profit or any other commercial damages, including but not limited to special, incidental, consequential, personal, or other damages.

Image credits:

The chapter heading images in this book were created using DALL-E, an AI program developed by OpenAI. These images are AI-generated and, as such, are not subject to traditional copyright, they are considered to be in the public domain. We acknowledge OpenAI and their DALL-E program for their role in creating these images.

Book Cover by Celeste Avonly

First edition 2024

Contents

Introduction ... 1
    Part 1: Personal, Interpersonal, and Emotional Life Skills

1. Mirror, Mirror on the Wall ... 6
    - Get To Know Yourself
    - Develop Emotional Awareness
    - The Emotional First Aid Kit

2. The Power of Body Language and First Impressions ... 16
    - Decoding the Non-Verbal Mystery of Body Language
    - Deciphering the World of Facial Expressions
    - The Good, the Bad, and the Awkward Gestures
    - Make A Great First Impression

3. The Art of Conversation ... 29
    - Listening: Taking the Art of Body Language to a New Level
    - Small Talk Isn't So Small After All
    - From Awkward Pauses to Fluid Dialogues
    - Phone Call Etiquette

4. The Kindness Paradigm ... 44
    - The Ripple Effect of Kindness
    - Empathy and Compassion
    - High School Drama and How to Rise Above It

5. Stress Less, Live More ... 56

    Understanding Stress: Physiology and Psychology
    Stress Management Strategies
    Mindfulness: The Stress-Busting Superpower
    Your Personal Stress Management Plan

6. Bounce Back, Soar High: Unleash Your Inner Resilience   67
    The Power of Resilience
    Build Your Resilience Muscle
    Your Personal Resilience Plan

7. Fueling Your Dreams: The Power of Sleep and Nutrition for Teens   82
    Sleep: More Important Than You Think
    The Sleep vs. Stress Seesaw
    The Teen's Guide to Nutrition
    Part 2: Practical and Technical Life Skills

8. The Balancing Act: Time Management   97
    Make the Most of 24 Hours
    Prioritize Like a Boss
    The Art of Saying No
    Your Personal Time Management Plan

9. Living In An Online World   112
    Understand Your Digital Footprint
    Manage Your Digital Footprint
    Protect Your Online Privacy
    Digital Detox: Unplug for a Healthier You

10. Show Me the Money   120
    Checking and Savings Basics
    Income vs. Expenses
    Saving for the Rainy Day: True Financial Responsibility
    Create a Workable Budget
    Building Financial Credit

      Real-Life Money Scenarios and How to Handle Them

11. Shop Right - Cook Right - Eat Right   135
    Meal Planning
    Grocery Shopping
    Meal Prep Like a Pro

12. Keep It Clean, Please   145
    Declutter Your Space To Simplify Your Life
    Organizing: Where Everything Has a Place
    Laundry 101
    Clean It Like You Mean It
    Part 3: Next Level Skills: Setting Goals, Getting a Job, and Adulting Like a Pro

13. Crafting Your Future   157
    The Power of Decision Making
    Setting SMART Goals
    Dream Mapping and Vision Boards
    Embrace Change: The Only Constant

14. The Path to Employment   170
    Landing Your First Job
    Building a Resume and the Application Process
    The Job Interview
    Explore Career Paths

15. The DIY Guide to Master Adulting   177
    Home Maintenance
    Basic Car Maintenance and Handling
    Navigating Public Transportation
    Paying and Filing Taxes
    Personal Maintenance

Conclusion   187

Companion Books by Celeste Avonly 191

References 192

Introduction

I definitely wasn't one of the popular kids in high school. I wasn't a total nerd either. I was just an average schmo trying to get in, get the job done, get by unnoticed, and get out. I spent a lot of my high school career getting credit for working, which meant I could get out of school early and make money while I was at it. Growing up, my parents always provided everything I needed, but they certainly didn't have money to spare, so if there was anything I wanted on top of my needs, I had to figure out a way to get it on my own. I started babysitting for money when I was 11 years old, which taught me the skills and know-how that enabled me to buy my own car when I turned 16, travel Europe at 17, and buy my first home just before I turned 20.

I'm the fourth child out of five, so I was frequently left to my own devices and often had to figure things out for myself. I was very shy and would consider myself slightly socially awkward as a teenager. I always had plenty of friends, but often did or said things that, looking back, were pretty cringe-worthy. However, I reflect on my childhood very positively, and all in all, I would say I had it pretty good. As an adult, I recognize that my experiences of childhood and adolescence led me to be a very self-sufficient and independent person who would no longer be considered shy by my peers. I'm grateful for the things I had to learn independently, but I would have loved to have a mentor to help me through some of the rough spots.

Now, as a mother, I feel my most significant duty is to be that mentor to my children. My goal is to teach them all the things I had to figure out on my own so they can go on to be successful humans who can contribute to their families and to society in a positive way. Watching my firstborn go from a bullied middle schooler to a confident, charming, outgoing, mr.-popular-college-man has been one of my greatest joys. As I continue to teach and guide my youngest, I've seen him blossom and grow before my eyes, and it's thrilling to watch. I'm not a high-class expert and I don't have a degree in raising humans, but what I do have is a growth mindset that has served me well, and plenty of life experience.

In this book, I hope to act as your mentor of sorts. We're going to tackle real-life challenges that teens face every day, from learning how to communicate and improve your social skills, to managing time and money (like a boss). We'll talk about becoming resilient and stress-free, and even how to eat and sleep so your brain and muscles can function at their best. We'll cover things like how and why to do your laundry and clean your bathroom, as well as setting goals and getting a job. We'll break down these big, scary topics into bite-sized, digestible chunks, using quick and simple activities and even a few role plays so you can confidently step into the adult world.

The information in this book is progressive and divided into 3 parts. We'll start with personal, interpersonal, and emotional skills - the skills everyone needs to be self-aware and interact with others every day. These skills include things like how to have conversations, kindness and empathy, stress management and resilience, and basic sleep and nutrition needs. Then we'll talk about practical and technical skills like managing your time, and money, and how to cook and clean. Finally, we'll touch upon higher level skills like goal setting, getting a job, and true adulting skills like home and car maintenance and taxes (blech).

There's a lot of information in this book, and the last thing I want for you is to be overwhelmed by it. My approach is always to take baby steps: become aware, learn the smallest, most doable part of the skill that you can manage, and practice what you're able to practice. Once you master one thing, move on to something new. I've included several activities and role-plays throughout the book, most of which are in part 1. Before you roll your eyes at role-plays (cause I hate them too), just remember that it doesn't have to be weird, and there are only a few of them. (If you're a parent reading this, you can easily sneak in role-plays any time!) At the very least, practice over and over in your mind, but at best, pick a friend, sibling, or parent and read out the role-play so they can understand what you're trying to accomplish. I often sit next to my kids and walk them through situations before they're faced with them in real life. This is such an essential step in creating confidence in a new skill, and I highly encourage you to try it out for yourself.

There are two ways I recommend reading this book. You can read it straight through from front to back, without pausing to work on the exercises (because even just having the information in mind will help you), and then go back and read through the chapters one by one to work through the exercises and learn the subject well. Or you can take your time and go through each chapter, do the exercises, learn the subject well, practice, and then master the skill before moving on to the next chapter. It all depends on you - there's no wrong way.

I've created a companion workbook that's available on Amazon if you want an organized place to work through the activities. Throughout this book, I'll tell you which page to find each activity within the workbook. However, the workbook is an added bonus, and I'm confident that even simply reading this book all the way through will help you with awareness, and boost confidence in learning these skills. You can find the workbook here:

Well I'm excited! Are you? Let's go!

A note to parents: I love to read through books like this *with* my children. I would encourage you to read through a chapter each night, or each week, with your child(ren), and work on the activities together. Not only is this a great way to bond with your teenager, but you'll also know exactly how and when you can help and support them. There may be some activities that your teen will want to be left alone to do, and it's important to honor that, but other activities are wonderful if done together as a family. Of course, do what's best for you and your family; either way, I hope this book is helpful to your teen. I'm excited for you to see them learn, grow, and thrive!

Part 1: Personal, Interpersonal, and Emotional Life Skills

In part 1 of this book, you'll learn about the fundamentals of personal, interpersonal, and emotional life skills. We'll focus on creating awareness and honing new skills so you can become the best version of yourself. This section is a guide to self-discovery, empathy, resilience, stress management, and creating meaningful and lasting relationships.

Chapter 1

Mirror, Mirror on the Wall

What I'm about to say will be repeated throughout this book and is the first step to fully understanding anything. That is being *aware*. Awareness of self, awareness of others, awareness of situations. What does it mean to be aware? It means you're paying attention.

But first: Self-awareness. Self-awareness is at the core of being a successful human.

If you show up to class with bed head because you didn't look in the mirror that morning, so you're not even *aware* your hair is sticking out in every which way, well, you only have yourself to blame for all the looks and laughs you'll be getting. (In an ideal world, you wouldn't get looks or laughs, but we know how it goes.)

If you're constantly putting people down and then wonder why no one wants to be your friend, it's time to become better aware of how and what you're saying to people.

Awareness is a fundamental skill that will improve over time and with practice. Everything you learn in this book will always start with expanding your awareness.

So, to get us started on what's arguably the most essential step to success in life, we'll do a few self-reflection exercises. This is your first opportunity of many to take out a piece of paper, grab your workbook, or open your phone to a new note (like, for real - don't skip out on doing the exercises), and let's do this.

Get To Know Yourself

Who Am I?

Okay, we're going to get right to work here with several exercises. Let's start with a question: Who am I?

The question "Who am I?" serves as a gateway to self-discovery, inviting you to explore the intricate landscape of your identity. It feels like a simple question, right? However, it might prove more challenging than you think. This question has no right or wrong answer; it's more of an exploratory exercise.

So, with your paper out, grab your phone and set a timer to 2 minutes, and without overthinking it, jot down words that resonate with you. Whether you're energetic or laid-back, outgoing or introverted, funny or serious, these descriptors are the building blocks of your self-perception. Don't judge your responses; let the words flow. After the 2 minutes, reflect on your list. How do these words make you feel? What aspects do you appreciate, and are there areas you might wish to transform? This exercise is all about fostering self-awareness, creating a blueprint that unravels the layers of who you are. The companion workbook will offer an alternative approach to this exercise, so refer to that if you have it (page 11). Remember, this is an exercise in creating awareness and getting to know exactly who you are.

Feeling stuck? Here are some prompts: Are you energetic or laid-back? Outgoing or introverted? Funny or serious? Happy or sad? Positive or negative? A morning person or a night owl? Musical or athletic? Compassionate, humble, smart, shy, ... Keep going!

What's My Jam?

Moving right along! Remember when you were a kid, and you'd get so lost in an activity that you'd completely lose track of time? Maybe it was painting, playing with Legos, or perhaps it was using your imagination while jumping on the tramp or dancing like nobody's business. That's what we call being 'in the zone'.

Fast forward to now. What activities, hobbies, or tasks get you 'in the zone'? It could be coding a new app, playing the guitar, or even solving complex math problems (hey, no judgment here!). These are the things that make you tick, the things that light a fire in your soul. They're your jam!

So, let's get to it. If you have the workbook, go to page 15. Otherwise, grab your paper and write down at least five activities that you absolutely love doing. The ones that make you forget to check your phone, ignore your growling stomach and lose track of time.

(Yep - go do it right now.)

Take a look at the activities you just wrote down. These are activities that can lead to true happiness in life, a purpose, or a fulfilling career. I encourage you to fully explore these activities and learn what you can about each of them. We'll dig deeper into this later on in the book.

Remember that you always reserve the right to change your mind; new things can become your jam anytime. Learning and exploring new things are the beauty of life!

What Makes Me Tick?

Now, this part is like peeling an onion. We're going to delve deeper into understanding what drives you. Above, you wrote down what you do, but this exercise is not about *what* you do but *why* you do it. It's about the values, passions, and motivations that fuel your actions.

For example, if you love playing basketball, is it the thrill of competition that drives you? Or is it the camaraderie and teamwork? Or maybe it's the sheer joy of perfecting your three-point shot.

Similarly, if you enjoy volunteering at the local animal shelter, is it because you love animals? Is it because you believe in giving back to the community? Or is it the satisfaction of making a difference, however small?

See where I'm going with this? The *what* is important, but the *why* is what really makes you YOU.

So, take those activities you listed in the "What's My Jam?" exercise, and for each one, write down two to four reasons *why* you love doing it. Dig deep. You might surprise yourself with what you discover.

And there you go! You're off to a solid start toward understanding yourself. Remember, this isn't a one-time thing. You're constantly evolving, and so is your understanding of yourself, so revisit these exercises occasionally.

Keep exploring, keep questioning, and most importantly, keep being your awesome self! Oscar Wilde once said, "Be yourself; everyone else is already taken." And he couldn't have been more right.

Develop Emotional Awareness

Developing emotional awareness, or understanding your emotions, is an integral part of being self-aware, and learning skills to navigate your emotions is one of the most essential tools in your life skills toolbox. Good emotional awareness will help you have more self-esteem and build better relationships. Sometimes, emotions are seen as the villains in your story. In fact, they're more like misunderstood superheroes trying to tell you something important, so don't be so quick to judge yourself if you're highly emotional.

Decode Your Emotions

Think of emotions as your body's way of communicating with you. It's like your body has its own unique language, and your emotions are the words. Sometimes, it whispers with a gentle feeling of contentment, and other times, it screams with a wave of anger.

The key to understanding this language is to decode your emotions. Start by naming the emotion you're feeling. It could be happiness, sadness, anger, fear, surprise, or disgust. These are six of the core emotions that all of us experience.

Next, try to figure out what triggered the emotion. Was it something someone said? Or was it a memory that popped up? Maybe it was something you saw or heard.

Finally, pay attention to how your body reacts to the emotion. Do you feel a knot in your stomach? Is your heart pounding? Are your palms sweaty?

Now, take out your workbook (page 17), phone, or paper, and let's write down one or two of your personal, real-life examples. Think of a specific experience you had that triggered a big emotional response, and write down what that experience was. Next, write down one of the core emotions from above that was triggered by that experience. Finally, write down what you remember feeling in your body while experiencing that emotion; how did your body react?

If you can't think of a specific example, remember to do this exercise the next time you have a remarkable emotional experience, and notice how your body reacts.

Doing this exercise can help you understand what your emotions are trying to tell you. The way your body responds to an emotion can tell a story of past experiences, including happy memories or even trauma. Sometimes, you will notice the bodily response before you decode the emotion or feeling behind it. So once you understand how an emotion manifests within your body, you can work to enhance or change those reactions in a way that suits you best.

For example, if you feel fear every time you take a test and you start to shake and sweat, once you are fully aware that is how your body responds to tests, you can work to overcome that fear and bodily response. Likewise, if you feel happiness every time you visit grandma's house and your heart starts to flutter, and you start to shake, you can recognize that your body might respond to happiness and fear similarly. This can help you reframe emotions and situations so you have a more preferred response in the future.

We'll talk more later about how your thoughts influence your emotions and how you can change an emotion by changing your thoughts - that's an upperclassman skill. For now, let's continue on with becoming emotionally aware.

The Feelings Thermometer Activity

Picture a thermometer in your mind. Instead of measuring temperature, this one measures the intensity of your emotions. At the bottom is calm, and at the top is the most intense emotion you can imagine.

Now, think of a situation that made you feel an intense emotion. It could be the anger you felt when your friend canceled plans at the last minute or the joy you felt when you aced that test you were worried about. Or maybe when your sibling ate the last piece of pizza you were saving or when your crush texted you back.

Place this emotion on your feelings thermometer. Was it a boiling-over-the-top kind of emotion? Was it a lukewarm-in-the-middle type? Or was it a cool-and-calm-at-the-bottom emotion? What experiences bring out the biggest emotional responses? Write those down (page 19 in the workbook).

By visualizing your emotions this way, you can better understand how different situations affect you emotionally. Other people will react to the same experience in different ways, and that's perfectly okay! The key is to know how *you* respond to a situation. Emotions make life colorful and interesting and add depth to our existence, so strong emotions aren't always a bad thing.

Riding the Emotional Rollercoaster

Imagine you're on a rollercoaster, and it's the wildest ride of your life. You're zooming up to dizzying heights and then plunging into thrilling lows. You're feeling a whirlwind of emotions, from exhilaration and joy to fear and anticipation. Now, imagine that this rollercoaster ride is your emotional life. That's pretty intense. Also pretty normal for any teenager.

Consider keeping an "emotional rollercoaster" diary of sorts. It's like a travelog of your emotional landscape, a record of your inner rollercoaster ride. Every day, jot down the emotions you experienced, the situations that triggered them, and where they fell on your feelings thermometer. You can find this exercise on page 21 of the workbook.

Did you start the day feeling energized and excited, only to feel stressed and overwhelmed by lunchtime? Did a text from a friend lift your spirits in the afternoon, only for a challenging homework assignment to bring you down in the evening?

You'll start noticing patterns and trends by keeping track of these emotional ups and downs. You may find that certain people, situations, or even times of the day tend to trigger specific emotions. Or you'll discover that your emotions fluctuate more than you realized. You can make it easy by keeping an emotion log in the notes section of your phone, or there's a page in the workbook to help you keep track. Go ahead and track it for a week or three and see what you find.

***

So, let's put it all together. By doing these activities, you're not only understanding your emotions, but you're also a step closer to being able to manage them. Remember, your emotions are not your enemies but your allies. They're a vital part of who you are, and understanding them is a big step towards understanding yourself. So, the next time you find yourself reacting to something with a big emotion or feel like you're on an emotional rollercoaster, remember to tune in, decode, and listen. Your emotions have much to say, and it's all worth hearing.

The Emotional First Aid Kit

Now you're a pro at detecting your emotions (being aware!), but what can you do about them when they start to feel like too much? Well, we've all heard of a first aid kit, right? It's that box filled with band-aids, antiseptics, and other stuff to patch us up when we have a physical injury. But what about when we're dealing with emotional bumps and bruises? That's where the "emotional first aid kit" comes in.

Your emotional first aid kit is a personalized set of tools and strategies to help you cope when you're experiencing intense or complex emotions. It might include things like:

- Deep breathing exercises for when you're feeling stressed or anxious.

- A playlist of uplifting songs for when you're feeling down.

- A list of people you can reach out to when you're feeling lonely or overwhelmed.

- A set of affirmations to boost your confidence when you're doubting yourself.

- A favorite book, movie, or video game that helps you relax and unwind.

Remember, what works for someone else might not work for you, and that's totally okay. Your emotional first aid kit should be tailored to your needs, preferences, and what you find effective. If something else has worked for you in the past, make a note of that and practice it regularly.

Right now, I want you to take a minute and look through these options or think of something that has worked for you before, and choose one or two you can practice. Don't just expect to be able to recall and make it happen the next time you're feeling emotionally charged - you need to know and practice your response in advance. Take some time right now to figure it out. Take a few minutes to see what it's like to practice deep breathing, set up a playlist of songs on your phone, or write down people you can reach out to, words you might recite, or a list of books or other activities to help you calm down. Determine what you feel could work for you and write them down (page 25 in the workbook). Having different plans for different situations can be helpful. You may be unable to start listening to music while you're under pressure taking a test. However, you can most definitely take some calming deep breaths or recite some affirmations silently in your mind.

Sometimes, when you're in the middle of big emotions, having someone else who can guide you in the right direction to calm down is helpful. My youngest son's favorite calming activity is to jump on the trampoline. My oldest likes to listen to music and has several playlists to influence the mood he's going for. We both know this works for them, so I can nudge them in that direction when I know they need it. Once you've figured out what works for you, tell your parents, siblings, or friends so they can help you when you're right in the middle of those big emotions.

The Emotionally Charged Role-Play

Oh boy, here it is - the first role-play. This one only has one actor - you - so humor me, k?

Have you ever wished you could have a do-over for a situation that didn't go as planned? Maybe you lost your cool during an argument or froze up when you were put on the spot. We've all been there.

That's what the "Emotionally Charged" role plays are all about. You get to replay those situations in a safe and controlled way and experiment with different responses.

Here's how it works. Think of a recent situation that charged up your emotions. Now, replay that situation in your mind, but imagine responding differently this time.

Maybe you take a few deep breaths before responding to the argument. Or you could use a coping strategy from your emotional first aid kit when you're on the spot.

By practicing different responses, you learn more about your emotions and build a repertoire of strategies for navigating emotionally charged situations. It's like rehearsing for a play, but the play is your life, and you're the star of the show.

That was easy, right? You're now equipped with tools and strategies to navigate the wild ride of emotions. Practice, practice, and soon enough, responding intentionally to emotions will become second nature. You've got this!

Chapter 2

The Power of Body Language and First Impressions

Have you ever realized how much you can communicate even without speaking a single word? Yep. Even when your lips are sealed, your body is blabbering away like a podcast host on a caffeine buzz. There's a whole silent world of non-verbal communication that conveys emotions and intentions beyond the reach of words. And it's called body language.

Your body language is your unspoken vocabulary; it's as vast and colorful as the English language itself. Every move you make sends out a message: from the tilt of your head to the tap of your foot. Just as much as you need to be able to "read" the messages others are sending with their body language, you need to be aware of the messages you're sending with yours. But here's the catch - this unspoken vocabulary doesn't come with a dictionary where you can look up defined meanings. Bummer, right?

It's okay - I've got your back. We will decode this non-verbal mystery together, and by the end of this chapter, you'll be fluent in the language of body talk. You'll be able to figure out what others are trying to say with theirs, as well as be mindful of the things you're saying with yours. So let's get started!

Decoding the Non-Verbal Mystery of Body Language

Become a Body Language Detective

Alright, Sherlock, it's time to put your detective hat on. Your mission, should you choose to accept it (I know - different movie..), is to observe the body language of the people around you. You could do this anywhere - at home, school, or even while hanging out with friends.

Here's how it works. Without being creepy or invasive, casually observe how people use their body language. Notice their posture, gestures, facial expressions, and even the way they use personal space. Try to decode what their body language is saying. Is your teacher's crossed arms and furrowed brow a sign of annoyance? Does your friend's constant foot tapping mean they're nervous?

Keep an open mind as you do this because body language can be subjective, and it's important not to jump to conclusions. The aim of this game is to sharpen your observational skills and develop your understanding of non-verbal cues. Remember what I said in Chapter 1? It all goes back to becoming *aware*.

Spend a bit of intentional time every day taking notice and then trying to figure out what people around you are saying with their body language. It's okay if you get it wrong, just start becoming observant and aware, just like a detective would.

The Silent Signals Scavenger Hunt

Okay, here we go! Another activity! Once again, use the notes section on your phone, grab a piece of paper you can hang on to, or use the companion workbook (page 29). We're going on a scavenger hunt! The goal is to identify and interpret different types of body language in real life or the media.

First, create a list of body language cues. Things that you noticed as a body language detective, like a confident stance, a nervous fidget, finger tapping, or an engaged nod. Write down 10 to 15 body language cues. Then, for a week, try to spot these silent signals in the people around you or in characters on TV shows and movies. Jot down where you saw the signal, then write down what you think it meant in that context.

This scavenger hunt will not only make you more aware of the different ways body language is used, but it will also help you become better at interpreting these silent signals.

In the process of observing others, you'll become more aware of your own body language. As you get better at understanding body language as a whole, you'll find that you're improving your communication skills and also gaining deeper insights into the thoughts and feelings of others. And that, my friend, is a superpower! So keep practicing, stay curious, and remember that communication is about so much more than words.

The Non-Verbal No-Nos

While it's important to be comfortable expressing yourself in the way you see fit, there are certain long-standing social "rules" that can make or break your social game. There are several non-verbal "no-nos" to be mindful of. These are body language blunders that can send the wrong message and can give people a negative impression of you or your character. Let's dive into some of the most common ones:

- Avoiding Eye Contact. This can make you seem disinterested or dishonest. Eye contact is a sign of engagement and sincerity. Holding eye contact can be extremely hard for some people, so it's important not to judge too harshly if someone struggles with this. However, if *you* struggle to maintain eye contact, practicing and increasing time spent making eye contact is absolutely a skill you can learn and become comfortable with over time.

- Slouching. This can make you appear lazy, lacking in confidence (and bullies tend to go after kids lacking in confidence), or disinterested. Stand or sit up straight to project an image of self-assuredness.

- Crossing Arms. This can create a barrier and make you seem defensive or closed off. Keep your arms relaxed at your sides or use them to gesture while speaking.

- Fidgeting. This can be distracting and can signal nervousness or impatience, so try to keep your movements calm and controlled.

- Sighing. This can convey frustration, impatience, or annoyance and may be perceived as disrespectful or dismissive. If you need to take a deep breath, ensure the rest of your body language is engaging and positive.

Keeping this list in the back of your mind can help you avoid these non-verbal no-nos and ensure your body language sends the right message. Take what you learned about self-awareness in Chapter 1 and apply it here. Pay attention to your body language and decode what you're saying even when you're not saying anything.

Deciphering the World of Facial Expressions

Now, let's zoom in on a crucial aspect of body language – facial expressions. Think of your face as the billboard of emotions; it's often the first thing people notice and a direct way to show how you feel.

A smile, for instance, is universal. It can bridge gaps, convey friendliness, and lighten the mood. But not all smiles are created equal. A genuine smile crinkles the corner of your eyes, radiating warmth and sincerity. On the flip side, a forced smile might just involve the mouth and can come across as insincere. If you've ever heard the term "smile with your eyes", that's speaking of a warm, genuine smile that shows across the whole of your face.

They say the eyes are the window to the soul, and that is very much true. Your eyes can express a myriad of emotions. Wide, bright eyes often show excitement or interest, while a furrowed brow and narrowed eyes might convey confusion or suspicion. And of course, there's power in making eye contact – it can show confidence, interest, or even challenge.

Your eyebrows play a significant role too. Raised eyebrows can signal surprise or disbelief, while furrowed eyebrows might show concern or concentration.

Your mouth and nose also join in this non-verbal dance. A tightened jaw can signal tension or anger, and flared nostrils might signal irritation or aggression.

But here's the tricky part – facial expressions can be as nuanced as a complex language. Context is key. A smile in one situation might convey happiness, while in another it might be masking discomfort. That's why it's essential to look at the whole picture – the setting, the body language, and the facial expressions as a collective.

So start observing – not just others, but also yourself. Notice how your face reacts in difference situations. Do you frown when concentrating? Do your eyes light up when you talk about something you love? Understanding your own facial expressions helps you manage them better but also learn to express yourself more effectively.

The Good, the Bad, and the Awkward Gestures

Gestures are also considered body language, but are defined as specific, *intentional* movements of hands, arms, or body parts. They're like punctuation marks in your non-verbal conversation, adding emphasis and clarity or sometimes causing a whole lot of confusion.

There's the friendly wave that bridges distances, the reassuring pat on the back, clapping to show appreciation, excitement or agreement, and the celebratory fist pump.

Then there's the too-firm handshake that borders on aggression (a firm handshake is a great thing, though! Just keep it civil), the pointed finger that implies blame, or the middle finger that's, uh... well, rude. These gestures can often unintentionally create invisible barriers, hindering communication and understanding. Again, awareness is key. Understanding the impact of our movements allows us to navigate social landscapes with finesse.

Sometimes our well-intentioned gestures become *awkward* gestures. You know those moments when a gesture doesn't land as expected? Maybe you went for a high-five, and they went for a fist bump. You used air quotes and a confused look was shot back. Or you tried to wave at someone, but they didn't notice, and you had to style it out. It's okay! We've all been there.

Here are some tips to help you sidestep these cringe-worthy moments and help you feel less awkward in social situations:

- Consider the context: Some gestures are more appropriate in certain situations. A thumbs-up might be okay among friends but might not be the best choice in a formal setting.

- Mirror the other person: When in doubt, follow the other person's lead. If they offer a handshake, respond with a handshake. If they're using a lot of gestures, feel free to do the same. If they're not using a lot of gestures, maybe dial down your own use.

- Try to avoid using the same gestures over and over.

- Practice making eye contact as much as possible, even if it feels uncomfortable for you. Just don't turn it into a staring contest – it's perfectly okay to look away every once in awhile. Not making any eye contact is awkward in social situations, as is starting people down.

- Holding something in your hands or keeping your hands in your pockets can help you avoid fidgeting or gesturing awkwardly.

- When in Rome: Be aware of cultural differences in body language. What's considered polite in one culture might be regarded as rude in another. And remember, cultures certainly differ worldwide, but they may also vary from family to family within your community. Use those detective skills to determine what's appropriate and what might be considered rude.

Everyone has awkward moments from time to time, so don't stress too much about it. The key is to learn from these experiences and handle them with a dash of humor and a whole lot of grace. Laughing at yourself can be the best way to smooth over an awkward situation and move on with your life.

Body Language Charades

Now, we're going to put it all together. You've played the game of charades, right? I suggest a slightly different version for you to play now. Get your friends or family together and have some fun with this. You could even do this in front of a mirror by yourself.

Here's how it works. Choose a simple story or scenario. It could be something as straightforward as "I woke up late, rushed to get ready, and barely made it to the bus stop in time." Now, tell this story using only body language. No words, just gestures, expressions, and movements. Ask your friends or family to guess the story based on your body language. You'll be surprised at how much you can express without saying a word!

Another way you could do this is each day when you get home from school, tell your mom how school went by using body language, expressions, and gestures only. She'll love to get more out of you than "my day was fine."! Doing this daily is a great way to practice and ensure your body language is on point and sends the message you want it to.

Understanding body language is a continuous learning process, but being aware of the messages you're sending when you're not saying anything at all will help you in all aspects of your life. So stay curious, keep practicing, and most importantly, have fun with it!

Make A Great First Impression

A first impression is the initial perception or judgement we make about a person the very first time we meet them. First impressions are crucial because they lay the groundwork for future interactions and can shape how a relationship develops. So now that you're a body language pro, here's a pop quiz: when you meet someone for the very first time, how long do you think it takes to form a first impression? A minute? Thirty seconds?

Try a tenth of a second. Yikes! That's quicker than a blink of an eye! But within that fraction of a moment, the human brain rapidly processes facial expressions, body language, and overall demeanor, forming snap judgments that can significantly influence how we perceive others. And here's the clincher - although they *can* change over time, first impressions tend to stick, so we want them to be as positive as possible!

It can be scary to think that in a blink, people are forming judgments about your character, trustworthiness, and even your social status based on your appearance, body language, and expressions. Sounds unfair, right? It might be, but it's a natural part of how humans interact. This rapid judgment process served our ancestors well as they navigated unknown territories and encountered strangers. Today, in our fast-paced world, these split-second assessments shape our interactions and influence our decisions, often before a single word is spoken.

Understanding this phenomenon will help you be more mindful of your body language and expressions, and maybe even how you choose to do your hair, or the clothes you wear.

Being aware of this process can give you confidence to let people know the type of person you truly are from your first meeting. You can make a positive first impression by smiling, being confident, friendly, and genuine when you meet someone new. This will be especially helpful when you're interviewing for a job, or you want to set the stage as an "A student" the first time you meet a new teacher. Remember, even though first impressions happen fast, they CAN change as people get to know you better, so don't despair if you feel you've made a wrong first impression in the past. Let's talk about some ways you can work towards making a great first impression.

Build Confidence In Yourself

Some of you are probably shy, have been bullied, or struggle hard with interacting with others. I hope to inspire you by telling you a little story about my oldest son, who is now 21 years old and in college. He may remember it differently, but to me, this was the advice given to him that changed the course of his life.

We moved to a new home the summer before he started middle school. Any way you slice it, middle school is rough, but being the new kid adds insult to injury. He was shy and not at all confident in talking to other kids. It didn't take long before he started getting bullied - just a little bit - at school. Other kids would poke at him, say mean things, and laugh behind his back, and he wasn't making any friends. As mama bears often do, I had to find a way to intervene.

I asked him about his body language while walking the halls at school. Did he keep his head up? Did he look people in the eyes? Did he smile? Or did he keep his head down and just try to go unnoticed from one class to the next? As suspected, he walked with his head down to avoid eye contact and keep others from bothering him. Well, the shy, unconfident kids are the biggest targets of bullies, and his body language was screaming a lack of confidence.

We worked on baby steps. For one week, I told him to try walking the halls with his head held high. The deal was he didn't have to look at anyone or say anything, but he needed to look confident. Fake it til you make it. He did.

In week two, he was to keep his head high and add in a smile. That's it - just smile. He did.

In week three, he added saying a simple "hi." It didn't matter who he said hi to, and he wasn't required to say anything beyond that. This was a hard one for him, but he practiced and did it.

Once he felt a little more comfortable saying hi, I encouraged him to choose one or two people he knew and say hi with their names. Every week, he added a couple people to say hi to with their name. I also encouraged him to learn new people's names and say hi to them. Once he felt comfortable with that, we worked on eye contact while he said hi.

He kept working hard at these simple steps, and astonishingly, by the time he reached high school, this kid was confident enough to get involved in things like student government, and he was easily described as outgoing and an extrovert. A complete 180 from where he had been just two years prior. Now he's in college, and he's the glue that holds his friends together; he is outgoing and in his element when helping others feel liked and included.

I was also very shy as a kid, so I understand how crippling that can feel. I didn't have a mentor to help guide me through how to get beyond my shyness. I just thought that was how I was going to be forever. If you feel this way, please know that you can be a valued and wonderful person, whether you're shy or outgoing. You don't have to change a thing.

However, if you feel crippled by your shyness, just as I did, and you want to overcome that, you absolutely can. The saying "fake it til you make it" works, and there's nothing wrong with doing it. Practice exuding confidence, and before you know it, you'll feel confident for real.

Build A Confident First Impression

So whether you're shy, or outgoing and the life of the party, take a moment to reflect on how you make first impressions and what you might want to change or improve upon. Go ahead: think through it for a minute or two.

Now it's time to take out that paper or notes section on your phone or your workbook (page 33) and write down a few baby steps you could take to make a better first impression. Is it your body language? Maybe checking your hair every morning before leaving for school. Or perhaps it's starting with basic interactions like my son did. Write out 3-5 small, simple steps that might feel like a little stretch but are absolutely doable for you. Work on those steps one at a time until you're comfortable enough to move on.

Every time you meet someone new, reflect on the impressions you feel you made and come back to this exercise until you feel confident that your first impressions are telling people exactly what you want them to know about you.

The Elevator Pitch

The elevator pitch is something you'll hear about in business, but there's no reason you can't learn it now. It's a very intentional "first impression" you can practice in advance.

Imagine you're in an elevator with your dream employer or college admissions officer. You only have the time it takes for the elevator to go from the 1st floor to the 8th floor to introduce yourself and make a strong impression - maybe only 30 seconds or so. An elevator pitch is like a mini-speech you prepare in advance to make the most of that brief moment. It's a way to quickly tell someone who you are, what interests you, and what you have to offer. Think of it as a chance to shine brightly in a very short amount of time. An effective elevator pitch is concise, compelling, and authentic. It's not about boasting or hard-selling; it's about sharing who you are. If you have a good elevator pitch ready you can seize unexpected opportunities to leave a lasting impression on people you meet, especially in professional or academic situations, but also in less formal situations where someone might ask you about yourself.

So, take some time right now to craft your elevator pitch (page 35 in the workbook). Get help from family and friends if you need it. Write down who you are, what you're interested in, and some of your strengths. Write down variations until it's about the right length (you can read it in 30 seconds) and it sounds natural. Once you have a pitch you're happy with, practice it regularly until it feels natural and genuine so you can easily recall it when the right moment arises. Make changes to your elevator pitch whenever you think changes are warranted. Remember, confidence is key!

The Power Pose Workout

The final tip for making a solid first impression is comin' in hot, and this one is fun! Ever heard of a power pose? This is where you get to be the star of your own superhero movie! Power poses are all about using body language to boost your confidence and command presence. This isn't something you'd do in front of other people, but something you'd do *before* any situation where you'd need confidence or a boost to self-esteem.

Think about all those superheroes and their poses while looking over the city from the top of a tall building. Each superhero has their own power pose - can you think of what they are? In many, feet are apart, hands are on the hips, back is tall, chest is out, shoulders are back, and chin is up. Now, think about how *you* stand when you're feeling confident. Are your shoulders back, your chest open, and you're standing tall? That's a power pose.

Standing in a power pose, even for just a couple of minutes a day, can make you feel more powerful and self-assured. It's like your body telling your brain to feel strong and capable. Kind of like how athletes might pump themselves up before a big game. But instead of shouting, like an athlete might do, you're using the power of body language.

So, here's your workout. Each day, spend two minutes in a power pose – just two minutes is all you need. Definitely do this before a big presentation, a test at school, a job interview, or even a first date. It's a quick and effective way to boost your confidence and make a solid first impression.

The science behind first impressions might seem daunting, but with all of these tools and strategies, you can make the best of those crucial first moments. Remember, first impressions aren't about pretending to be someone you're not. It's about presenting the best version of yourself with confidence and authenticity. Keep practicing, stay true to yourself, and you'll be a pro at making stellar first impressions in no time!

Chapter 3

The Art of Conversation

Conversations are like the Wi-Fi of social life; they connect us. They're how we share stories, express ideas, and build relationships. But let's be real; they can also be as tricky as catching a slippery fish with your bare hands. You've got to know when to talk, when to listen, what to say, and how to say it. It's like performing a perfectly choreographed dance and hoping you don't step on anyone's toes in the process. This chapter is your dance lesson. By the end, you'll be waltzing your way through every conversation, from chit-chat at the lunch table to heart-to-hearts with your closest pals.

Listening: Taking the Art of Body Language to a New Level

We're going to tune into one of the most underrated aspects of body language: the art of actively listening.

Imagine you're at a concert. The band is on fire, the crowd is going wild, but you've got earphones on, and you're listening to a podcast. You might be hearing some of the music, but you're completely missing out on the show, right? That's what conversations feel like when you're distracted and not actively listening. You're there, you might be getting some bits of the conversation, but you're not soaking in the melodies of meaningful dialogues. So, let's figure out how to take your listening skills to a new level.

Gauge Your Listening Skills

Here's another pop quiz! This is about helping you gauge your listening skills, so there's no need to write anything down. Just give yourself an honest answer.

1. When someone is talking to you, do you put your phone away?

2. When someone is talking to you, do you make eye contact?

3. Do you refrain from interrupting when someone else is speaking?

4. Can you recall details from a conversation you had earlier in the day?

5. Do you respond with empathy when someone shares their feelings with you?

6. Do you ask follow-up questions during a conversation to show interest?

7. Can you paraphrase what someone just said to you?

Be honest with your answers - remember, it's all about becoming *aware* of what you are currently doing and then improving what you see needs to be improved.

Mastering the art of active listening is a valuable skill that can improve your relationships and understanding of the world around you. Here are several tips to level up your listening game:

- Start by being present in the moment. That means stop thinking about other things and give all your attention to the conversation you're having.

- Put away distractions, like your phone, and don't get distracted by things going on around you. Again, give your full attention to the speaker.

- Maintain eye contact, as it not only shows respect but also helps you grasp the speaker's emotions. But remember to blink and keep a friendly facial expression.

- Engage in the conversation by asking questions and providing verbal and non-verbal cues, demonstrating that you are fully attentive (remember your body language, expressions, and gestures training).

- Cultivate empathy by putting yourself in the other person's shoes and trying to understand their feelings and perspectives. Make it about them, not about you.

- Patience is key - let them finish their thoughts before responding. Take note of *their* non-verbal cues like body language and tone of voice, as emotions are often conveyed more profoundly than words. With practice, it will become easier and like second nature to be the G.O.A.T. at listening (for the adults in the room, that means Greatest Of All Time).

The Active Listening Role-Plays

Now, let's put theory into practice. You're going to do some active listening role-plays. This will be easy! Grab a parent, sibling, or friend and get into character. One of you will play the speaker, and the other the listener. The speaker shares a story or an experience, and the listener's job is to actively listen.

Remember, active listening is more than just not saying anything. It's about showing interest, understanding the message, and responding appropriately. So, as the listener, remember to make eye contact, nod occasionally to show you're following along, and give verbal affirmations like "Uh-huh" or "I see." Respond with empathy, ask relevant questions, and provide feedback by paraphrasing what the speaker said.

Once you're done, switch roles and repeat. After both rounds, share feedback with each other. What did you do well? What could you do better? Role-plays like these are perfect for honing your listening skills in a safe, supportive environment. If this role-play feels too awkward for you, move on to the "silent conversations challenge" below and practice, practice, practice!

The Silent Conversations Challenge

We're going to take it to a whole new level now. I call it the silent conversations challenge. For one whole day, try to spend more time listening than speaking in every conversation. If you're a talker like me, this is definitely harder than it sounds, but trust me, it's a game-changer.

By choosing to listen more, you're not only showing respect to the other person, you're also learning more about them. You're opening yourself up to new perspectives, ideas, and stories. Plus, you're training yourself to be more patient, empathetic, and understanding.

So, take up the silent conversations challenge. It might feel tough initially, but stick with it, and you'll start noticing the incredible impact of genuinely listening.

Small Talk Isn't So Small After All

Ok, now that you're a pro at listening, let's move on to a more back-and-forth conversation style: small talk. Small talk is a casual conversation about light topics such as the weather, sports, or current events. Small talk gets a bad rap, but it's actually the secret sauce of social interactions. It's like the pre-game warm-up before the big match. It breaks the ice, sets the tone, and paves the way for deeper conversations. It can be awkward at first, but it's an important skill to learn because it can help you make friends, network with new people, and even help you get ahead in your career.

The Small Talk Topics List

First things first, you need to stock up on some top-notch small talk topics. Think of these as your conversation starters, your go-to subjects to kick-start a chat. Here's a quick list to get you started:

- The weather: Yeah, it's cliché, but it works! Everyone experiences the weather, so it's a common ground for everyone.

- School: Classes, teachers, homework, extracurricular activities.

- Music: Favorite bands, artists or songs. Music is a universal language.

- Sports: Whether you're a player or a fan, sports can generate some lively discussions.

- Books: If you're a bookworm, discussing your latest read could spark a fascinating conversation.

- Movies and T.V.: Current favorites or upcoming releases. What's the next binge?

- Current events: Stay informed about what's happening in the world, and you'll never run out of things to talk about.

General social rules say to stay away from talking about politics and religion, so unless you're sure those topics won't start a heated discussion, it's probably best to keep them off your list of conversation starters. Otherwise, can you think of any other topics you can add to the list above?

It's important to remember that small talk is not a competition. It's not about trying to be the most interesting or intelligent person in the room. It's simply about getting to know someone better and making a connection.

The Conversation Starter Cards

Next, let's turn these topics into actual conversation starters. This is a great exercise that will help you remember some simple conversation starters when you need them most. If you're a more hands-on learner, grab some index cards or small pieces of paper; otherwise, open your phone to a new note and copy down the following bullet list. There's also a page to write these down in the companion workbook (page 37).

- "Have you seen the latest episode of [popular T.V. show]?"
- I'm looking for a new show to binge-watch. What have you been watching?
- "I heard [band/artist] 's new song on the radio. Have you heard it?"
- "I can't believe how hot/cold it's been lately."
- "Did you catch the [local sports team] 's game last night?"
- Are you planning on going to the game this weekend?
- "I just finished reading [book]. Have you read it?"

- What did you think of the homework we had yesterday?

Add more to the list as you think of them. Writing these down will help you better recall them when you need to start a conversation or fill an awkward pause. You can even keep this list or your notecards handy and review them before going into a social situation so you have some ideas at the ready.

Real Life Small Talk Scenarios

Small talk isn't just about filling the silence; it's about building connections and getting an engaging conversation going. It's the first step in getting to know someone, and knowing how to start up conversations will reduce a lot of social awkwardness. To illustrate this, let's look at a couple small-talk, big-impact scenarios.

Scenario 1: You're at a school event and spot a new student standing alone. You walk over and comment on the weather. The new student agrees and mentions they're not used to the cold weather because they just moved from a warmer state. Boom! You've just learned something new about them, and you can steer the conversation towards their experiences in their previous hometown.

Now let's pretend the person responded with a simple "yeah. it's cold". Keep trying with a different small-talk conversation starter until you find something the person will want to engage in conversation about.

Scenario 2: You're at a family gathering and seated next to your music-loving cousin. You mention the latest song you heard on the radio. Your cousin's eyes light up, and they start talking about the band and how they've been following their music for years. Voila! You've just turned a casual chat into a passionate discussion. Use the information you already know about someone to start up a conversation.

These scenarios show how small talk can lead to deeper, more meaningful conversations, which is the ultimate goal. So, the next time you're stuck in a small talk situation, remember - it's just the starting point of a journey into a deeper conversation and getting to know the person you're talking to better. So embrace it, enjoy it, and let the chat flow!

From Awkward Pauses to Fluid Dialogues

So, here's the thing. Conversations are a lot like playing catch. You toss the ball, they throw it back, and the game goes on. But sometimes, the ball drops, and you're left with... well, an awkward pause. It's like forgetting your lines during a play: awkward and maybe a little embarrassing, but not the end of the world. So fear not, my friend, I've got your back.

The Awkward Pause Survival Guide

Picture this. You're at a party, you've employed your small talk conversation starters, and now you're chatting up a storm with someone you've just met. The conversation is flowing like a river, and then bam! Out of nowhere, an awkward pause ambushes you. You can hear the proverbial crickets chirping as you scramble to find something, anything, to say.

Has this happened to you? If it hasn't yet, it likely will.

Here's the secret. Awkward pauses are only as awkward as you make them. It's all about your perception. Think of them as breathers, little islands of silence in the river of conversation. They give you a moment to gather your thoughts, process what's been said, and decide on the route the conversation should take next. You could face the awkwardness head-on with a little bit of humor by mentioning it and laughing about it. Something along the lines of "Well, this is an awkward pause." Or you can pull out your conversation starter cards (don't literally pull them out - THAT would be awkward!). Think about what you practiced, pick up the conversation with a new cue, and start over: "So, are you going to the game this weekend?" There, convo saved.

The next time you hit an awkward pause, don't panic. Take a deep breath, embrace the silence, and then pick up the ball and toss it back into the game. It's as simple as that, especially if you've practiced your conversation starters!

Sometimes you might feel like all you're doing is going through your conversation starters one-by-one. So let's talk about keeping the conversation ball rolling. It's all about the flow, the back-and-forth exchange that makes a conversation feel like a dance. If you're struggling with getting a conversation really going, don't sweat it; here are some handy conversation flow tips to turn you into a smooth talker:

- First up, be curious. Genuine interest in the other person is the fuel that keeps the conversation engine running. Ask open-ended questions (those are questions that aren't answered by a "yes" or "no"), delve into topics they seem passionate about, and show enthusiasm for their stories and ideas. Remember faking it til you make it? This can apply here too. Even if you don't feel truly interested in, say, the dog they seem to want to talk about, show interest anyway. You might actually learn something new.

- Second, remember, it's a two-way street. A conversation isn't a monologue. Make sure to balance speaking and listening. Share about yourself, but also give them space to express their thoughts and experiences. Find a connection, or a common interest and pause every once in awhile while speaking so they have a turn to say something too.

- Finally, go with the flow. Conversations are unpredictable, and that's what makes them exciting. Don't stick to a script. Be open to twists and turns, and be willing to explore new topics as they pop up.

The Smooth Talker Challenge

Ready for a challenge that will help you put everything into practice and become the G.O.A.T. at conversations? The task is simple: over the next week, make it a point to strike up a conversation with someone new every day. It could be a classmate you've never spoken to, a neighbor, your bus driver, or even the girl at the check-out counter where you're buying lunch. If you're nervous, try a power pose in advance, practice in your mind what you're going to say, and fake the confidence if you have to!

Use the conversation starter cards from our small talk toolkit and the conversation flow tips from above to keep the chat going. If you hit an awkward pause, use it as a breather and dive back in.

By the end of the week, you'll notice you're becoming more comfortable starting and maintaining conversations. You'll find it easier to navigate awkward pauses and keep the conversation rolling. And who knows, you might even enjoy the thrill of these spontaneous chats! Remember, like any skill, it takes practice to get better at conversations. So, get out there, strike up a chat, embrace the awkward pauses, and let the conversations flow.

Phone Call Etiquette

Now that we've got the conversational ball rolling, it's time to change gears and delve into a topic that's often overlooked but incredibly important - phone call etiquette. Yes, in the age of texting and social media, good old phone calls still hold a place of importance. So hit the pause button on texting and tweeting for just a second, and let's go old-school, back to the days when phones were for, well, making phone calls. You know, those voice-to-voice, ear-to-ear exchanges that happen in real-time. Scary, right? But don't break a sweat because I promise that if you can get past the scariness of making a phone call, you just might be the one to get all the dates, and you'll definitely be held in high regard by "the older generation," which could land you a better job.

Making phone calls is scary for almost anyone, but it becomes easier and easier with practice. You just have to do it.

Way back in the 1900s, when my husband and I were first married (calm down - it was 1997), you had to actually call everyone for everything. Like, the internet was new and didn't do much except help you research things or chat with strangers in public chat rooms. I know - weird. My husband and I were legit adults, but we were married young and weren't used to doing many things on our own - like calling for pizza. Before the days of ordering everything online, you had to actually call the pizza place and tell them your order over the phone. For whatever reason, it was stressful. Well, guess what? If we wanted pizza, we had to adult up and call to order pizza. So we did. We also had to make phone calls to make all our appointments, to hire plumbers or to talk to a banker. Yes, it was always a little stressful initially, but it became no big deal with practice.

As I learned, making phone calls was stressful for most of my adult friends too - most people feel the same way – it's totally relatable. Over time, the friends that made the phone calls became less afraid of it. But I've also watched friends let others always make phone calls for them, and for those friends, it's still a scary thing, even in their 40s.

So when my oldest was a young teenager, I decided he needed to learn how to make phone calls on his own, even though by then, you could pretty much do everything over the internet or text. We always started with writing everything down that he would need to say so he was prepared (this is key and something I highly recommend - I'll teach you how to do it a little later). I have been amazed at how he has honed this skill over time. He prefers to call girls to ask them out, something most boys in H.S. and college don't do (spoiler alert - girls love him for it), and he makes all his appointments independently, which is an essential life skill. This skill has also helped him many times in his various jobs (in fact, his current job is medical translating... done over the phone).

All it takes is practice. I can't say that enough. You will always be afraid of it if you don't do it.

The Phone Faux Pas List

There are some don'ts of making phone calls that we need to go over before we dive into the do's. Consider this your "phone faux pas" list - the NOT-to-do list of phone calls. You'll notice it's very similar to having a face-to-face conversation.

- Don't multitask. Sure, you're a pro at juggling tasks, but when you're on a call, give it your full attention. No one likes to compete with background noise or feel like they're on the back burner.

- Don't over-talk. Remember, a phone call is a two-way street. Don't hog the conversation; give the other person a chance to speak.

- Don't under-talk. On the flip side, don't leave the other person hanging. If you're too quiet, they might think you've been abducted by aliens or fallen into a black hole.

- Don't shout. Unless you're lost in a jungle and trying to signal a rescue helicopter, there's no need to yell. Speak in a normal, clear voice.

By steering clear of these faux pas, you're already ahead of the game. Now, let's move on to the phone call DO list.

How To Make A Phone Call

- Prepare for the call. This is what I was talking about above. Before you make a call, think about what you want to say. Have all the relevant information you might need written down. For example, if you're ordering pizza, write down exactly what you want to order. If you're making an appointment, write down your insurance information (or have your insurance card right in front of you) and any other information you might need for your specific appointment. If you will be using a credit card over the phone, have the credit card in front of you. For your first several phone calls, go ahead and write down what you want to say, word-for-word, so you can simply read it off. You'll have to do this less and less as you get used to talking to someone over the phone.

- Be aware of your surroundings. Don't make a phone call when there's a lot of noise around.

- Use a hands-free device. This will allow you to hear as well as possible and prevent muffled sounds from your end.

- Be polite and professional. Actually smile. You can tell when a person is smiling - it makes your voice sound more friendly and approachable. Greet the person on the other end of the line with a friendly tone. Introduce yourself and state the purpose of your call.

- Speak clearly and slowly. Avoid using slang or jargon (don't say things like: "Sup! Hit me up with a large pepperoni 'za with some fire wings and a side of ranch, brah!"). Speak slowly and enunciate your words so the person can understand you clearly.

- Be an active listener: when the person on the other end is talking, pay attention and even take notes so you can remember what they said.

- Be concise and to the point. Get to the point of your call quickly and avoid rambling. This is where those word-for-word preparation notes come in handy.

- Thank the person for their time. Before you end the call, thank the person for their time, and if you need to follow up, let them know when and how you will do so.

If you need help, don't hesitate to ask a parent, another trusted adult, or a friend for assistance. I always stood right next to my son when he was making phone calls in case he needed some coaching or had a question he didn't know how to answer. Having someone nearby can help reduce a lot of anxiety.

Phone Call Practice Role-Plays

It's time to put your phone call skills to the test with some phone call practice role-plays. Grab a friend and get into character. One of you will be the caller, and the other will be the receiver.

The caller's task is to make a phone call with a specific purpose. Maybe you're calling to make a dentist appointment, ask for homework help, or even chat about the latest episode of your favorite show.

The receiver's job is to respond appropriately, keeping the phone faux pas list in mind. After the call, switch roles and repeat. Give each other feedback on what worked well and what could be improved. And don't forget to just have fun with this!

Remember, the only way you get better is to practice. The more you practice, the more comfortable and confident you'll become in making and receiving phone calls. When you're ready to make that first real phone call, use page 39 in the workbook to help you prepare.

The Text vs. Call Debate

Let's address the elephant in the room - the text vs. call debate. When is it appropriate to call, and when is a text message enough? Here's a simple rule of thumb:

- When clarity or an immediate response is needed, a phone call is your best bet. It allows for real-time clarification and leaves less room for misinterpretation.

- When the information is straightforward and non-urgent, a text message will do the trick. It's convenient and allows the other person to respond at their own pace.

Of course, there are exceptions to every rule, and different situations call for different modes of communication. The key is to consider the context, the urgency, and the personal preferences of the person you're communicating with.

Here are a few situations you might want to consider making a phone call instead of sending a text:

- Anytime you need to have a serious conversation. Texting is not always the best way to have a serious discussion, especially if it's a difficult one. It can be hard to convey tone and emotion over text, and it can be easy to misunderstand each other.

- To make a request. If you're asking someone for something, it's always best to do it over the phone. This shows that you are serious about your request and willing to put in the effort to have a conversation about it.

- To apologize. If you have done something wrong, it is important to apologize sincerely. A phone call is a more personal way to apologize than a text.

- To show gratitude. If someone has done something nice for you, expressing gratitude is always a good idea. Another great way to show gratitude more personally than a text is to record a video of yourself thanking the person and send it to them over text.

I encourage you to challenge yourself with this. Phone calls can be very scary, but I'll keep saying it - the only way to overcome the fear of making a phone call is to do it, and then do it again and again.

Chapter 4

The Kindness Paradigm

To finish out the section on relationships, we're going to talk about kindness, empathy, and a little bit of drama. Kindness is a virtue that is important to uphold. It is a way of showing respect for others and demonstrating our shared humanity. Kindness is a basic human need. It's also contagious. When we are kind to others, it inspires them to be kind to others as well. Kindness is a powerful force for good. Showing kindness has a positive impact not only on your own life but also on the lives of others. It can improve mental health, strengthen relationships, help you succeed in school and work, and help create a more positive and compassionate world. In the world of social media, where it's easy to post anonymous comments without taking responsibility for our words, kindness is as important a skill as ever to learn and practice.

The Ripple Effect of Kindness

Imagine you're at the beach, you pick up a pebble and toss it into the sea. It causes a tiny splash, right? But then, you notice the ripples. They start small, right where the pebble hit the water, and then they spread out, wider and wider, reaching far beyond the point of impact. Kindness works in the same exact way. It may seem small, like that pebble. Still, its impact creates ripples that reach far and wide, touching lives and transforming communities, even if you don't always see the effects firsthand.

Impact on Personal Relationships

Kindness should always start with the people closest to us - our friends and family. Have you ever noticed how one small act of kindness can change the whole vibe of your home? Maybe you help your younger sibling with math homework or surprise your parents by cleaning up the kitchen. It's a small gesture, but it speaks volumes. It says, "I care about you." It fosters a sense of love, respect, and mutual support, which are the building blocks of solid relationships.

Showing kindness to a family member can be as simple as helping your little brother tie his shoelaces. Or maybe your mom's had a long day - offering to cook dinner or even help out a little bit could be just the relief she needs. Perhaps your grandpa feels lonely - chatting with him about his youth could brighten his day.

Now, think about your friends. Imagine you're having a bad day, and your best friend shows up with your favorite snack, just because. That simple act of kindness not only lifts your mood but also strengthens your bond with your friend.

These acts of kindness are like a soothing balm, bringing comfort, joy, and a sense of togetherness. Overall, kindness makes relationships more enjoyable and fulfilling. We feel loved, supported, and appreciated when surrounded by kind people. This makes our relationships more positive and rewarding.

Influence on School Environment

Now, let's take those ripples of kindness into your school. Schools are like mini societies, bustling with diverse individuals, each with their unique personalities, backgrounds, and experiences. Imagine what would happen if kindness became the common language in this vibrant society.

You share your notes with a classmate who was absent due to sickness. A group of seniors volunteer to mentor the freshmen. The basketball team helps to clean up the schoolyard after a big game. Or, someone might be having a bad day - a few kind words or a friendly smile can make a world of difference. These acts help create an environment of cooperation, respect, and mutual support.

The impact? A positive and inclusive school culture where every student feels valued and respected. It decreases bullying, improves student relationships, and even boosts academic performance. These acts of kindness don't require a grand gesture or a heroic effort. They're about noticing the people around you, understanding their needs, and taking that small step to lend a hand. It's like turning your school into a well-knit community where everyone looks out for each other, and it can all start with just one person - you.

Effect on Community Cohesion

Let's take it up a notch and look at the bigger picture - the community. Communities are like puzzles, made up of unique pieces, but all fit together to create a beautiful picture. Kindness is like the invisible force that holds these pieces together.

Think about it. You take part in a neighborhood clean-up drive. A local business offers free lunches to the homeless. A group of residents organize a fundraiser for a family in need. These acts of kindness not only solve immediate problems but also bring people together, encouraging a sense of unity and shared responsibility.

The result? A cohesive community where people care for each other and work together for the common good. It makes the community a better place to live, fostering a sense of belonging and mutual respect among residents. It's like turning your community into one big family bound by the ties of kindness.

That's how the ripple effect of kindness works - it spreads from personal relationships to schools to communities, but it always starts with just one person. Just like that pebble at the beach, your small act of kindness can create waves of positive change.

Spread Kindness

So here's my challenge to you: toss a pebble - choose a small act of kindness you feel comfortable doing, and go for it. It doesn't have to be something significant and life-changing; in fact, the smallest acts of kindness often feel more genuine and end up having the most significant effects. Let your kindness ripple out into the world. You'll feel better for it, and those you show kindness to will undoubtedly be grateful.

It's time to go into action. Take out your phone, paper, or workbook (page 41). I encourage you to write down ideas that are coming to you for ways to show kindness. If an idea comes, don't judge it; just write it down. Once you have a list, work through it at your own pace, but also pay attention to opportunities that might arise to show someone a little bit of kindness.

Below, I'll share some ideas if you're ready for something bigger. The point here is to show kindness and compassion, period. But as a bonus, don't forget to look into your school's graduation requirements to see if some of your acts of kindness might work towards graduation. Have cake; eat it too.

Initiate a School-Wide Kindness Project

Ever thought about how amazing it would be to turn your school into a kindness zone? Where every corridor echoes with friendly greetings, every classroom buzzes with cooperative learning, and every lunch break brims with inclusive conversations. Sounds like a dream, right? But guess what? You can turn this dream into reality with a school-wide kindness project.

Start with brainstorming. Gather like-minded friends and think of ways to infuse kindness into your school's daily routine. It could be setting up a compliment box where students can leave anonymous compliments for each other. Or maybe a 'buddy system' where older students mentor younger ones. Or how about a 'random acts of kindness' week where everyone is encouraged to do something kind for someone else?

Once you've got your idea, it's time to plan and execute. Seek support from teachers and school administrators. Rally your fellow students and get them excited about the project. Remember, the goal is to create a positive ripple effect throughout the school. So, lead with enthusiasm, persistence, and, of course, kindness.

Organize a Community Service Event

Let's take our kindness wave outside the school and into the community. Organizing a community service event is a fantastic way to spread kindness and positively impact your local community. Plus, it's an excellent opportunity to unite people and foster unity and cooperation.

Again, start with brainstorming. What does your community need? A clean-up drive in the local park? A fundraising event for a local charity? A free tutoring program for underprivileged kids? The possibilities are endless. Choose a project that resonates with you and aligns with the needs of your community.

Next, plan your event. Recruit volunteers, gather resources, and spread the word. Don't think you have to go at it all alone! Bring your friends in on the action. On the day of the event, lead with enthusiasm, and remember to show appreciation for your volunteers' time and effort. After all, kindness is contagious, and your event could inspire others to carry the kindness torch forward.

Create a Kindness Journal

Finally, let's bring the kindness challenge home, quite literally, with a personal kindness journal. Find an empty journal you love and dedicate it as your acts of kindness journal. This is a space to record *your* acts of kindness, reflect on their impact, and brainstorm new ways to spread kindness. It's also a place to record acts of kindness you've *received* or even those you've *witnessed*. Reflect on how these acts made you and others feel. Over time, you'll have a beautiful record of kindness that will inspire you to keep the kindness wave rolling.

Creating a kindness journal is more than just an exercise in self-reflection. It's a reminder of the positive impact you can make on the world around you. It's a testament to the power of kindness and a motivation to keep spreading it, one small act at a time.

Empathy and Compassion

Picture yourself as a superhero for a moment. You've already got the perfect power pose, no? You're not a cape-wearing, crime-fighting kind (although that does sound pretty cool), you're the kind of superhero who wields the power to connect with people on a deep, emotional level. You can understand their feelings, respond compassionately, and build stronger, more meaningful connections. Sounds like a pretty impressive superpower, right? Well, guess what? It's called empathy, and you've already got it.

Empathy is the ability to understand and share the feelings of another person. It's a skill that everyone is born with, but it needs to be developed and practiced. Empathy is essential to building strong relationships, resolving conflict, and creating a more compassionate world.

Empathy is different from sympathy. Sympathy is feeling sorry for someone else. Empathy is understanding and sharing their feelings. Another way to think about empathy is to put yourself in someone else's shoes. Imagine that you are going through what they are going through.

Understanding Others' Perspectives

Imagine that you are walking down the street, and you see someone crying. You don't know why they are crying, but you feel a little bit sad yourself. That's empathy. You can understand and share the other person's feelings, even though you don't know their story.

Next, imagine standing in front of a painting in an art gallery. You're focused on the vibrant colors, the bold strokes, and the overall composition. Now, imagine stepping back and looking at the painting from different angles. Suddenly, you notice things you hadn't seen before - subtle shadows, hidden patterns, tiny details that add depth and complexity to the artwork.

That's what empathy is like. It's the ability to step back from our viewpoint and see things from another person's perspective. It's about stepping into their shoes and trying to understand their thoughts, feelings, and experiences.

How do you do this? By listening actively, observing non-verbal cues, and asking open-ended questions, all without judgment. You do it by showing genuine interest in the other person and making an effort to understand their worldview. It's not about agreeing or disagreeing with them but acknowledging and validating their feelings.

Emotional Responsiveness

Let's take the painting analogy a bit further. Now, imagine you're not just observing the painting, but you're also responding to it. You're moved by the colors, intrigued by the patterns, and touched by the emotion captured in the artwork. That's the next level of empathy - emotional responsiveness.

Emotional responsiveness is about not just understanding but also sharing the feelings of others. It's about feeling joy when they're happy, sadness when they're down, and frustration when they're struggling. It's about mirroring their emotions in a way that shows you're not just hearing their words but also feeling their feelings.

This doesn't mean you have to be an emotional sponge, soaking up everyone else's feelings. It's about showing empathy without losing yourself in the process. It's about being there for others without forgetting to be there for yourself.

Building Stronger Connections

Now, let's bring it all together. You've understood the other person's perspective and responded to their emotions, and now, you're ready to take the final step - building a stronger connection.

Empathy is an essential aspect of all relationships. It fosters trust, mutual respect, and a sense of closeness. It makes the other person feel seen, heard, and valued. It's like a bridge that connects two individuals, allowing for a free flow of communication, understanding, and mutual support.

When you show empathy, you're telling the other person, "I see you. I hear you. I understand you. I'm here for you." And that, my friend, is the most powerful message you can send to another human being.

High School Drama and How to Rise Above It

By now, you know how to build extraordinary relationships and show kindness and empathy to others, but it's time to spill the tea. You can only be in control of *you*. And while you may be doing your best to spread love and joy to those around you, despite your best efforts, high school remains a breeding ground for drama. It's like a reality TV show where the plot twists are as predictable as they are exhausting. Rumors spread faster than wildfire, friendships can turn into feuds in a heartbeat, and social media just adds fuel to the flames. But here's the catch - you don't have to get sucked into the drama vortex. You can use all your new skills to rise above it.

I feel this is important to mention because the teenage years are complicated, and everyone is trying to figure things out in their own time and space. Many of your friends and classmates are dealing with significant life problems that you likely have no idea about. Your job is to show kindness, but what do you do when others around you aren't doing the same? Sometimes, it's hard not to join the gossip train or think ill of someone because they think they're so fire for whatever reason. Well, I want you to keep the following in mind.

Drama Detox Challenge

Think of drama like junk food. It's addictive, it gives you a quick high, and it leaves you feeling empty and unsatisfied. What do you do when you want to kick a junk food habit? You go on a detox, and that's precisely what we will do with drama.

So, here's the challenge. For one week, try to consciously avoid drama. If you see a conflict brewing, steer clear. Gracefully bow out if someone tries to rope you into a gossip session. If you feel the urge to post a subtweet or a shady Instagram story, hit pause and reconsider. This can feel very hard to do, as being an insider on the current gossip can make you feel important and in the know. But rising above will help you feel even more powerful, and showing kindness where other may not be is endlessly more important in the long term.

This is not about being a pushover or avoiding genuine conflicts that need resolution. It's about choosing not to engage in pointless drama that drains your energy and adds no value to your life.

Role Models That Rise Above

Let's talk role models for a sec. I'm not talking about celebs or influencers with millions of followers. I'm talking about people in your life who handle drama like pros. You know, the ones who stay cool under pressure, who don't engage in gossip, and who handle conflicts with maturity and respect.

Identify at least three such people in your life. They could be friends, family members, teachers, or even characters from books or movies. Observe how they handle drama and conflict, and try to learn from them.

Maybe your big sister has a way of shutting down gossip without being rude. Or perhaps your favorite book character has a knack for resolving conflicts without losing their cool. These are the people who can show you how to be a drama-busting ninja!

Take out your notes or workbook (page 43) and write down two or three people who are role models to you, then write down the attributes they have that you would like to foster in yourself.

The Drama-Free Zone Blueprint

Keep that notebook out (page 45), and let's create a blueprint for a drama-free zone. This isn't a physical space but a mental and emotional one. It's about setting boundaries, nurturing positive relationships, and cultivating a drama-resistant mindset.

First, set boundaries. This means deciding what kind of behaviors you will and won't tolerate. It could be refusing to engage in gossip, not tolerating bullying, or not allowing others to drag you into their drama. Write down two to three drama-free boundaries you're committing to.

Next, nurture positive relationships. Surround yourself with people who lift you up, not those who drag you down into a sea of drama. Invest time and energy in friendships based on mutual respect, trust, and positivity. I tell my kids all the time that they don't need to be best friends with everyone, but they do need to be friendly to everyone. Yes, everyone. Make a list of friends that build you up and that you want to spend more time with because they are positive influences. Those friends that aren't the best influences? Well, maybe spending less time with them while maintaining your friendliness might be the best thing for you in the long run.

Lastly, cultivate a drama-resistant mindset. This is all about perspective. Instead of viewing drama as something exciting or engaging, see it for what it really is - a drain on your time, energy, and emotional well-being. Let alone how damaging it is for the person being gossiped about.

Thought it might not seem so right now, high school drama is just a tiny blip on your life's radar; once high school is over, you can leave it all behind. Remember, you can't control other people's behavior, but you can control *your response* to it. You can create your own drama-free zone by setting boundaries, nurturing positive relationships, and cultivating the right mindset.

***

And with that, it's a wrap on our deep dive into self-reflection, emotions, and building and nurturing relationships. You've unpacked some hefty topics, faced some challenging questions, and hopefully emerged with a clearer understanding of yourself and others. But remember, this is just the beginning. The road to mastery is long and full of twists, turns, and fascinating discoveries. So, just like I tell my kids, keep practicing because you'll never get any better unless you practice. Stay aware, keep exploring, keep learning, and most importantly, be yourself.

Chapter 5

Stress Less, Live More

Imagine that you're walking down a dark alleyway. You hear a growling noise behind you and you turn around to see a large dog running towards you. Your heart starts racing, your palms get sweaty, and your stomach flips. You have two choices: fight the dog or run away.

Now, swap that dog for a big test, the growling for a ticking clock, and you've got a pretty accurate representation of stress. It's your body's natural response to a challenge or threat, getting you ready to take action. But what happens when this stress becomes a constant companion? Let's break it down.

Understanding Stress: Physiology and Psychology

Fight, Flight or Freeze Response

The fight or flight response is a physiological reaction that occurs when you're faced with a perceived threat. It is a primitive response that has helped humans survive for centuries.

When your body perceives a threat, it releases a surge of adrenaline and other hormones. This causes your heart rate to increase, your breathing to speed up, and your muscles to tense. These changes prepare your body to either fight or flee the threat.

A less common response is the freeze response, also known as attentive immobility. This response is also a natural human reaction to danger. It is a temporary state of paralysis in which a person cannot move or speak. The freeze response is an evolutionary adaptation that helped us survive predators by avoiding detection. Teenagers may be more likely to experience the freeze response than adults because their brains are still developing.

The fight, flight, or freeze response is automatic and unconscious. You cannot control it. However, you can learn to manage these responses to stress, which we'll talk more about in the next section.

Chronic Stress and Health

What happens when you feel like everything around you is causing stress? Like you're stressing about an upcoming exam, worrying about a friend's problem, and losing sleep over a disagreement with your parents all in the same week, and the stress doesn't ever seem to let up. This is when stress moves from a protective, temporary response to a health hazard.

Chronic stress, or stress that's constant and prolonged can take a serious toll on your health. It can lead to headaches and sleep problems and even weaken your immune system, making you more susceptible to illness. It's like running your car engine on high gear for too long. Eventually, it's going to overheat and break down.

Stress and Cognitive Function

Now, let's talk about how stress affects your brain, the mission control center of your body. You know that feeling when your mind goes blank during a test? Or when you can't seem to focus no matter how hard you try? Yep, you guessed it - stress is the culprit.

All forms of stress trigger the release of hormones like cortisol and adrenaline. While these hormones are helpful in a fight or flight situation, they can wreak havoc on your cognitive function. They impair your memory, disrupt your focus, and can even affect your mood. It's like trying to navigate through a maze while blindfolded. No matter how hard you try, you can't seem to find your way.

So, it's clear that stress, especially when it's chronic, can be a real party pooper. It messes with your health, scrambles your brain, and generally makes life much harder. But here's the silver lining - you're not helpless. There are ways to manage stress, dial down the intensity, and make life more manageable. And that's precisely what we will explore in the upcoming sections.

Stress Management Strategies

Physical Activity and Stress Relief

Fun fact: Did you know that moving your body is like pushing a reset button for stress? When you exercise, your body releases endorphins, which are hormones that have mood-boosting and pain-relieving effects. Exercise can also help to reduce stress hormones, such as cortisol. Even a little bit of activity can make a big difference. For example, a study found that just 10 minutes of walking can reduce stress levels by 25%.

Other ways to move your body to reduce stress include:

- Yoga

- Dancing

- Playing sports

- Going for a walk or easy run

- Biking

- Swimming

- Hiking

- Pilates

- Tai chi

- Gardening

Any physical activity that you enjoy (that's key) can help to reduce stress.

One caveat here is that if you're under intense stress, pushing yourself too hard physically will only add to the stress hormones your body is already pumping out. If you're feeling really stressed, move your body, but make sure it's something more relaxing and soothing, like a walk, yoga, stretching, or a leisurely bike ride or swim.

Creative Outlets for Stress Reduction

On the flip side of movement is using your creativity. You know that feeling when you're so absorbed in painting a picture, strumming a guitar, or writing a poem that you forget all about that history test or that argument with your friend? That's creativity working its stress-reducing magic!

When you engage in creative activities, you enter a state of "flow" where your mind is fully engaged in what you're doing. It's like taking a mini-vacation from your stress, allowing your mind to relax and recharge. Plus, creative activities will enable you to express and process your emotions, which is a key part of managing stress.

There are so many ways to use your creativity to whisk you away into a stress-free state. My youngest son is still young enough to go to the land of imagination. When his stress levels are peaked, he'll enter his land of imagination and play dragons and swords. Instantly, he's forgotten what stressed him out so bad. My oldest son has organized his music playlist so he can listen to songs with just the right tempo to influence his body to a calmer state.

Here are some more ideas you could try:

- Art: Painting, drawing, sculpting, and other art forms can be a great way to express your emotions and relieve stress.

- Music: Playing an instrument, singing, or simply listening to music can be calming and relaxing.

- Writing: Writing in a journal, creating stories, or writing poems can help you process your thoughts and feelings healthily.

- Dance: Dancing is a great way to get exercise and express yourself creatively at the same time.

- Drama: Acting, improvisation, and other forms of drama can help you to develop your self-confidence and express yourself in new ways.

- Photography: Taking and editing photos can be a fun and creative way to capture the world around you and document your experiences.

- Cooking and baking: Working in the kitchen can be relaxing and rewarding. It can also be a great way to experiment with new flavors and ingredients.

- Gardening: Gardening is a great way to get some fresh air and sunshine, and it can also be very therapeutic to care for plants and watch them grow.

- Crafting: Crafting activities such as knitting, crocheting, sewing, and woodworking can be calming and relaxing. They can also help you create something beautiful you can be proud of.

Social Support and Stress Management

Lastly, let's talk about the people in your life - your friends, family, and even your favorite teachers. These folks are your social support network, and they play a crucial role in managing stress.

When you're feeling stressed, simply talking to someone you trust can make a huge difference. It allows you to vent, share your feelings, and gain a fresh perspective. Plus, knowing that you're not alone and that there are people who care about you and support you can make those stress monsters seem a lot less scary.

So, reach out to your friends, have a heart-to-heart with your parents or grandparents, or chat with a trusted teacher. It's okay to ask for support when you're feeling stressed! You don't have to face it alone. Remember, stress is a part of life, but it doesn't have to take over your life.

Mindfulness: The Stress-Busting Superpower

Pretend you're in the middle of a bustling city. Cars are honking, people are rushing past, and there's a whirlwind of activity all around. Now, imagine you've got a magic button. You press it, and suddenly, the noise fades away. You're still in the city but in your own peaceful bubble. Well, that's what mindfulness can do for you. It's your magic button in the chaotic city of life, helping you find your inner peace amidst the outer chaos. Mindfulness takes practice, but once you master it, you can tune anything out. It's not about completely escaping stress but learning to navigate it with grace and poise.

Mindful Breathing Exercises

Your mind is like a monkey, constantly swinging from branch to branch, never staying still for long. Mindful breathing is like a leash for your monkey mind. It helps you focus your attention on your breath and keep your mind from wandering. Mindful breathing is a simple but effective technique that can help you reduce stress, improve focus, and boost your well-being. Here's how you do it:

Find a comfortable spot. It could be a quiet room, a shady tree in the park, or even your favorite cushy chair. Close your eyes and take a deep breath in. Imagine that your breath is like a wave. It rises and falls naturally. As you breathe in, imagine that the wave is rising. As you breathe out, imagine that the wave is falling.

Now, focus on the physical sensation of breathing. Notice the feeling of the air entering and leaving your body. Notice the rise and fall of your chest.

As you breathe, try to clear your mind of all thoughts. If your mind wanders, that's totally normal; gently bring it back to your breath. Don't judge yourself or get frustrated if you find it difficult to focus on your breath. Just keep practicing, and it will become easier over time.

Start with just a few minutes of mindful breathing each day. Choose a time to practice this every day and work on deep breathing. As you get more comfortable with the practice, you can gradually increase the time you spend practicing. This is also a great thing to practice if you're struggling to sleep. Next time you're tossing and turning, give it a try!

Mindful Walking in Nature

Mindful walking is about turning a simple walk into a powerful stress-busting exercise. It's about experiencing nature with all your senses, grounding yourself in the here and now.

Find a natural setting, like a park, a garden, or a forest trail. As you walk, pay attention to the sensation of your feet touching the ground, the rhythm of your steps, and the sway of your body. Notice the sounds around you - the rustle of leaves, the chirp of birds, the whisper of the wind. Feel the sun on your skin, the earth beneath your feet, the breeze in your hair.

Doing this helps you slow down and de-stress and connects you with nature, reminding you of your place in the larger web of life. It's like plugging into a natural stress-relief outlet, recharging your mind, and rejuvenating your spirit. This is definitely my personal favorite way to de-stress!

Mindful Listening to Music

Finally, let's tune into the power of mindful listening. This isn't about just listening to music and letting go of your mind; it's about experiencing music in a whole new way, turning it into a stress-relief therapy.

As the music starts, close your eyes and let go of any distractions. Focus on the melody, the rhythm, the harmony. Notice the rise and fall of the notes, the interplay of instruments, and the emotions conveyed through the lyrics.

Feel the music flow through you, resonating with your heartbeat, vibrating in your veins. Let it take you on a journey away from stress towards peace and tranquility. It's like immersing yourself in a healing sound bath, washing away stress, and leaving you feeling refreshed and relaxed.

These are just three ways you can use mindfulness to help relieve stress. Try each of them out and see what works best for you.

Your Personal Stress Management Plan

Alright, now that you're armed with an arsenal of stress-busting strategies, let's put them to work. Consider this your blueprint for building a stronghold of resilience against stress. We're talking about creating a personalized stress management plan so you can conquer stress like a boss. Once again, get out your phone, paper, or workbook (page 47), and let's get to work!

Identify Stress Triggers

First up, we need to know the enemy. Stress triggers are the things that repeatedly get you worked up. They're like invisible tripwires: step on one, and boom - stress explosion. Triggers can be anything from a looming deadline, a difficult conversation, your math teacher, or even a cluttered room.

Think about your own personal triggers. Reflect on your day-to-day life, the times, places, and people that continually trigger stress inside your body, and jot these down. It could be any combination of situations, people, classes, or events that crank up your stress levels. As you go throughout your week, any time you are reminded of another stress trigger, write that down as well. When you're aware (there's that word again) of what stresses you out, you can make a better plan to mitigate the stress.

Select Effective Coping Strategies

Now that you've identified the triggers, let's arm ourselves with coping strategies. Remember the stress management strategies we talked about? Physical activity, creative outlets, social support, and mindfulness. These are your weapons against stress.

For each trigger, choose a strategy that you think will work best. Something you can employ as soon as possible in that type of stressful situation. If you're at home and a challenging homework assignment gets your stress levels soaring, maybe a brisk walk or a quick workout can help clear your mind. If a fight with a friend at school leaves you feeling stressed, perhaps some deep breaths at your desk or talking it out with another friend while walking the halls can provide some relief.

Remember, it's not one-size-fits-all. Choose strategies that resonate with you and fit into your lifestyle. It's about arming yourself with a toolkit of strategies that you can count on when stress strikes.

Regular Review and Adjustment of the Plan

Alright, you've identified your triggers and picked your strategies. Your stress management plan is ready to roll. But remember, this isn't a set-in-stone kind of deal. It's a living, breathing plan that evolves with you.

Make it a habit to review your plan regularly. Are the strategies working? Do you need to tweak them a bit? Maybe you've discovered new triggers or some old ones don't bother you anymore.

Adjust your plan as needed. Swap out strategies, add new ones, and remove triggers that are no longer relevant. It's about making the plan work for you, not vice versa.

Keep in mind that managing stress isn't about eliminating it altogether. It's about understanding it, taming it, and turning it into your ally rather than your enemy.

No matter how small, every step you take is a step towards a less stressed, healthier, happier you.

Chapter 6

Bounce Back, Soar High: Unleash Your Inner Resilience

Imagine you're building a tower of blocks. Just as you're about to add the final piece, your hand wobbles, and the whole tower comes crashing down. It's frustrating, right? But what do you do? You start over, perhaps with a sturdier foundation and better balance. You learn from the tumble and use it to build higher. This is a glimpse of resilience, and guess what? It's nestled within all of us, ready to be awakened.

The Power of Resilience

Resilience, in its simplest form, is the ability to bounce back from setbacks. It's about picking up the pieces after a fall, dusting yourself off, and moving forward. But here's the thing: resilience isn't just about recovery; it's also about growth. It's about learning from the stumble, adapting, and returning stronger, wiser, and more determined.

Think of resilience as a rubber band. When stretched or pulled, it doesn't just snap or break; it stretches and springs back to its original form. Similarly, resilience in us is that spring-like quality that helps us recover from life's pulls and pressures, bringing us back to our original form or, perhaps, an even better version of ourselves.

Benefits of Being Resilient

Resilience equips you to handle stress and adversity, and resilience fosters personal growth. Every stumble is a lesson, every setback a stepping stone. Resilience helps you extract the wisdom hidden in these challenging experiences, transforming them into stepping stones toward personal growth.

Resilience promotes optimism and boosts self-confidence. It's the voice that whispers, "You've got this," when you're faced with a daunting task. It's the belief that you can overcome, adapt, and grow, no matter what life throws at you.

For some, resilience might come easily, but for others, it might take more intentional effort. How resilient are *you*? What's your initial reaction when life doesn't go as planned? Do you want to quit, punch the wall, and never try again? (My youngest is naturally this way!) Or do you see it as a challenge, a learning experience, or a bump in the road? Don't get down if you struggle when things get tough - resilience can be nurtured; it just might be a little harder for some than others, and that's okay.

In the spirit of awareness, take out your notes or workbook (page 49) and write down how you typically respond to adversity in your life situations. Maybe you get angry and let it fester, punch the wall, or kick pillows. Or perhaps you're able to laugh at mistakes, think of what you could learn from the trial, or blow it off and forget it happened. Think through specific examples of when something stressed you out or when you made a mistake, and recall how you reacted in the several minutes or hours following. If you struggle with this exercise, it might be helpful to ask a parent, as they can typically see how you respond to adversity when sometimes it's hard for us to notice ourselves in that way.

Once you've written down a few examples, take a look and decide if you feel you're reasonably resilient or if you feel like this is a skill you could intentionally practice a little more.

Resilience in Action: Real-Life Examples

Let's look at resilience in action, in real-life scenarios, so you can get a good sense of how this works.

Picture yourself studying for a big test. You've spent days, even weeks, preparing. But when the results come out, they're not what you expected. You're disappointed, maybe even heartbroken. But here's an excellent opportunity to practice resilience. Instead of wallowing in disappointment, you take a deep breath, analyze your performance, identify areas of improvement, and start preparing for the next test. That's resilience.

Or, imagine you're trying out for the school's soccer team. You've practiced hard and given your best shot but didn't make the cut. It's a blow, no doubt. But instead of letting this setback crush your spirit, you view it as a temporary hurdle. You continue to practice, improve your skills, and try again next time. That's resilience.

Here's a personal story that's close to my heart. When my oldest started middle school (if you recall, middle school didn't start out very well for him), I made him join the cross country and track teams. He wasn't a runner before this, and he didn't want to be a runner now, but I told him he needed to participate in an after-school activity, and that's what he chose. At every practice, at every meet, he was dead last. My heart ached every time I watched him run, and the tears came easily. He told me he wanted to quit several times, but because he had committed at the beginning of the season, he wasn't allowed to quit (mom's rule). He had to see it through, and he did.

When he started high school, he did not join the track or cross country teams during his Freshman year. I couldn't blame him. But you know what happened? At the start of his Sophomore year, he realized that what he enjoyed from middle school was the team atmosphere, pushing his body, and working towards a goal. He looked past the fact that he was slow and not a natural runner, and he saw all the good that participating offered. He ended up joining the team Sophomore year. By the time he graduated, he had lettered in both track and cross country and had hit multiple personal records along the way (and was no longer dead last in any of his meets).

That's what a resilient attitude can do for you!

Remember, resilience isn't about never falling, but about rising each time you fall. It's about turning obstacles into opportunities and setbacks into comebacks. It's about embracing the tumble and then the climb, knowing that every fall just prepares you for a higher rise.

Now, let me share some of my favorite comeback stories. These are tales of individuals who stumbled and fell but refused to stay down. They rose and turned their failures into stepping stones towards incredible success. You've probably heard these stories before, but they're always worth repeating.

Thomas Edison

Let's travel back to the late 19th century to a humble workshop in New Jersey. Here's a man, hunched over a cluttered desk, eyes gleaming with determination. Meet Thomas Edison, the man who illuminated the world with his invention - the electric light bulb.

But here's the thing: this brilliant invention wasn't born overnight. Edison faced numerous failures, and countless experiments ended in disappointment. In fact, legend has it that it took him 10,000 attempts to create a functioning light bulb. Talk about persistence!

Through every failed experiment, Edison didn't see defeat. Instead, he famously said, "I have not failed. I've just found 10,000 ways that won't work." He viewed each setback as an opportunity to learn and improve. His resilience and refusal to give up in the face of failure eventually led to his groundbreaking invention that changed the world forever.

J.K. Rowling

Next, let's hop across the pond to the charming city of Edinburgh. In a quaint café, huddled over a worn-out notebook, we find a woman scribbling away with fervor. Meet J.K. Rowling, the creator of the magical world of Harry Potter, which is one of our families favorites of all favorites.

But the road to Hogwarts wasn't smooth. Rowling faced numerous challenges - from living on welfare as a single mother to dealing with multiple publishers' rejection of her manuscript. Yet, she didn't let these setbacks crush her spirit. She continued to believe in her story, relentlessly pursuing her passion for writing.

Rowling's resilience paid off when Bloomsbury Publishing gave her manuscript a chance. The rest, as they say, is history, and aren't we glad for it?! Today, she's one of the world's most successful and beloved authors, proving that resilience can turn even the most difficult situations into stories of extraordinary success.

Walt Disney

Finally, let's step into the enchanting world of animation. In a small animation studio in Kansas City, a young man is sketching his dreams. Meet Walt Disney, the man who brought us Mickey Mouse and the magical world of Disney (and another one of our families favorites – Disneyland!)

But before the magic, there was struggle. Disney faced numerous setbacks in his early career - from a failed animation company that left him bankrupt to the rejection of his early cartoon characters. But Disney didn't let these failures define him. Instead, he used them as fuel to work harder and dream bigger.

His resilience led him to create Mickey Mouse, a character that took the world by storm and marked the beginning of the Disney we know and love today. Disney said, "All the adversity I've had in my life, all my troubles and obstacles, have strengthened me... You may not realize it when it happens, but a kick in the teeth may be the best thing in the world for you."

Edison, Rowling, Disney - different people, different fields, but one common thread - resilience. They show us that failure is not the opposite of success but a part of it. They remind us that resilience is about bouncing back and growing through the process, and the potential that amazing things can come from the lessons we learn. So, the next time you face a setback, remember these stories. Remember that you, too, can turn your dreams into reality. All it takes is a little resilience.

Build Your Resilience Muscle

Develop a Positive Mindset

Let's talk about the mind. It's the control center of your resilience muscle. It sets the tone, lays the foundation, and calls the shots. A positive mindset is the fuel that powers your resilience engine. It's about viewing challenges not as insurmountable obstacles but as opportunities for growth.

But how do you cultivate a positive mindset? It starts with self-talk. That's right, the conversation you have with yourself in your head. If your self-talk is negative, you're essentially trying to drive with the parking brake on. It holds you back. So, flip the script. Focus on your strengths, celebrate your achievements, and remember past successes.

After positive self-talk, we need gratitude. Gratitude is the sun that illuminates even the darkest corners of your mind. Make it a habit to count your blessings, no matter how small. Keep a gratitude journal, or take a moment each day to reflect on something you're thankful for.

Finally, keep your eyes on the prize. Set realistic, achievable goals, and visualize yourself achieving them. It's like setting the GPS for your resilience journey. It gives you direction and focus, keeps you motivated, and fills you with a sense of purpose. We're going to talk a lot more about setting goals later on.

The Thought Model

This is an exercise I found years ago that has made all the difference to my family. This is the next-level guide for changing your thoughts and emotions to develop a positive mindset. I have taught the Thought Model to my children, and it's been amazing to watch them work through this process. In the beginning, they would struggle to change their thoughts and feelings (especially my youngest with

ADHD), but this model has been one of the most amazing tools in our toolbox and one I highly encourage you to use and practice regularly. It can seem pretty confusing at first, so you may want to enlist the help of an adult to work through it with you the first few times.

It goes like this:

→**Circumstances** are actual facts without emotion or bias. Something like, "I tripped on my shoelace and fell in the hall." It happened; it's just a fact. Circumstances can trigger thoughts.

↳**Thoughts** usually come into your head without warning due to the circumstance: "I'm so stupid! Everyone is going to laugh at me about this forever, and I never want to go to school again.".

↳Your thought will then cause a **Feeling**: "I'm so embarrassed!".

↳Your feelings cause **Actions**: "My face flushed, I ran away crying and didn't go to my next class."

↳Your actions cause **Results**: "You missed your next class and got behind on the homework as a result."

↩The results then provide evidence for our thoughts: "Now I'm behind on my homework and can't catch up. See? I'm so stupid."

See how that works? Take your time with this because it can seem confusing at first, but with time and practice, it will make perfect sense. On the following page is a visual I made, which might help it make more sense.

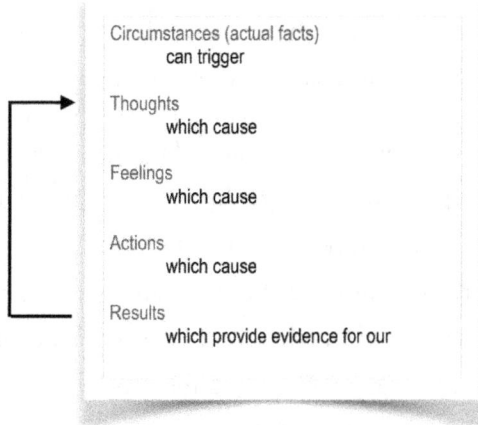

But here is the kicker to keep in mind. YOU are in control of *all* of your thoughts! They may come to your mind without warning, but you control how you respond to every thought. Every single one. Isn't that empowering?!

First, you must distinguish between a thought and a fact - they're very different. When you really start looking at things, you'll realize that most of your life is made up of thoughts surrounding a circumstance, not actual facts. It's the thoughts we have that make up how we perceive our life experiences.

So, if your thoughts cause your feelings and actions, and eventually create your results, isn't it nice to think that you can *think differently* to get a *different result*? Some thoughts are incredibly ingrained and will take more work to change, but if you want to, you can change every thought you have about anything and everything! And when you change your thoughts, you in turn change your emotions, feelings, actions, and results. Pretty amazing, right?

So the way this works is that when something happens that triggers a thought that doesn't serve you and just makes you want to punch the wall or quit, write down exactly what happened by completing an "Unintentional Thought Model." Start with the thought you had and write that down. Then, work backward and write down the circumstance that caused the thought (without bias - just the facts), and continue on to fill in the feelings you had, the actions you took, and the result of those actions. You can write this in a note on your phone or a piece of paper, or I've created empty thought models in the companion workbook (page 51) to help you visualize this easier. I know it can seem complicated at first.

Once you've written out your *Unintentional* Thought Model, you will create a new *Intentional* Thought Model, using a different thought for that same circumstance to produce a result that serves you better. For your intentional thought model, write down the circumstance first - because you know what happened there. Then write down a *new* thought - something different from what naturally came to mind before, but that will bring a more positive result. The key is to ensure this new thought feels genuine and true, even though it wasn't something that automatically came to mind. This takes practice, so keep trying! When you have a new thought picked out, fill out the rest of the model with the feeling, action, and result. Does it feel like that thought is the right one? If not, try again. Once you've practiced filling out some thought models a few times, changing the thought directly in your head will come more naturally instead of having to write it all out.

For parents: I work thought models on my kids regularly without them even really knowing that's what I'm doing. If they're being mad, sassy, or complaining, I help them develop a better thought that still feels true about the situation but will no longer make them feel like the world is out to get them. This has truly been one of the best things I've done as a parent, especially for my naturally pessimistic kiddo. It takes practice, but it's so worth it! There are books that teach this thoroughly, so if you're struggling, I encourage you to find a book and learn the ins and outs of how this works.

Build a Support Network

Okay, moving on with more ways of how to build your resilience muscle. Let's talk about the people closest to you. They're your pit crew in the race of life. They cheer you on, give you a boost when you're running low, and help you get back on track when you veer off course. Your support network is a crucial part of your resilience muscle.

Start with your family or those you trust the very most. They're your home base, your safe harbor in the stormy seas of life. Open up to them, share your challenges, and don't hesitate to ask for help. Their love, advice, and support can be a powerful resilience booster. You don't have to go at it alone.

Friends, too, play a crucial role. They're your teammates, running alongside you, sharing the highs and lows, and making the journey less daunting and more enjoyable. Surround yourself with positive, supportive friends who lift you up and inspire you to be your best self.

Don't forget mentors and role models. They're your guides, showing you the path, sharing their wisdom, and providing valuable insights from their journeys. Seek out individuals you admire, learn from their experiences, and let their resilience stories inspire your own.

Learn from Failures

The big f-word: *failure* (wink). Here's the secret - failure is not the enemy. In fact, it's one of your greatest allies in building resilience.

Think of failure as a teacher. Each mistake is a lesson, each setback a stepping stone. Instead of fearing failure or getting angry by it, embrace it. Analyze what went wrong, identify what you could do differently, and use it as a springboard to bounce back stronger and wiser.

Every successful person has a string of failures behind them. They're the battle scars of resilience, a testament to their courage, determination, and growth. So, the next time you fail, remember - it's not the end of the road but a stepping stone on the path to success and a chance to learn, grow, and become even better than before.

Practice Self-Care

We're still talking about building your resilience muscle here, and as part of that, we're going to touch just a little bit on self-care. Self-care is about caring for your physical, emotional, and mental well-being so you can stay strong, balanced, and ready to face life's challenges.

Physical self-care is about nourishing your body. Eat healthy, stay active, and get enough sleep. Your body is the vehicle for your resilience journey, and it needs regular fueling, servicing, and rest. We're going to go deeper into this later on.

Emotional self-care is about nurturing your heart. Express your feelings, build positive relationships, and engage in activities that bring you joy. Strive to have positive emotions as often as possible (tune in to those thoughts!) Positive relationships and emotions enhance your resilience and increase feelings of love, connection, and happiness.

Mental self-care is about stimulating your mind. Learn new things, practice mindfulness, and maintain a positive mindset. If your body is the vehicle for your resilience journey, your mind is the driver, and it needs regular challenges, relaxation, and positive reinforcement.

Resilience isn't just about bouncing back from challenges but also about preparing yourself to face them. And self-care is a crucial part of that preparation. So, take care of yourself because the benefits are plentiful!

Your Personal Resilience Plan

Resilience is your invisible armor, helping you stand strong in the face of adversity. But how do you equip this armor? How do you prepare for the battles that life may throw your way? The answer lies in creating a personal resilience plan. It's like your secret playbook, guiding you to handle setbacks with poise and bounce back with strength.

Identify Potential Setbacks

The first step in your resilience plan is anticipating the bumps on your road. These are your potential setbacks, the challenges that could rattle your journey. It could be a tough exam, a competitive sports event, or even a challenging group project.

At the beginning of this chapter, we did an exercise in awareness, so you should have already made a list of your potential setbacks (if you haven't yet, get out those notes or workbook and do it now). Look at your list again and add to it if something new has come to mind, then continue on.

Create a Plan of Action

Now that you've identified your potential setbacks, it's time to devise your action plan. This is your game plan, your step-by-step guide on how to deal with each setback.

Looking at your list, for each potential setback, consider the best way to handle it. If it's a tough exam, maybe your action plan includes a study schedule, extra tutoring sessions, or even a study group with friends. If it's a challenging group project, your action plan could consist of a clear division of tasks, regular progress checks, and open communication with your team. Maybe it's conflicts within a relationship. You could set clear boundaries for interacting with that person, take a time-out when a conversation starts to get heated, or maybe spend some quiet time deep breathing and meditating or working on a thought model. For my youngest, a common form of adversity in his life is just school in general. If he has a bad day, our plan for him is to take time after school to move his body - usually by jumping on the trampoline. In the winter, it might be a few minutes of quiet time in his room with his favorite book. These things help him recover from his "bad day" so he can return to school with a good attitude the next day.

Remember, your action plan should be realistic and practical. It's not about eliminating the setback but about managing it effectively. It's about turning the setback from a stumbling block into a stepping stone.

Take a minute to write down your plan of action next to each potential setback on your list (page 55 in the workbook).

Implement Your Plan

With your action plan in hand, you're ready to step onto the battlefield. This is where you put your plan... into action.

When a situation comes up in real life, remember that you planned and prepared for precisely this. Stick to your action plan as you navigate through each setback. Follow the steps you've laid out, but remember to stay flexible. Sometimes, situations may change, requiring you to adapt your plan.

Implementing your plan is like following a map on a treasure hunt. It guides you towards your goal, but sometimes, you may need to take detours or find alternate routes. The key is to stay focused on your goal, keep moving forward, and not see failures as a bigger setback but instead as an opportunity to improve.

Review and Adjust Your Plan

Finally, it's time to review and adjust your plan. This is your checkpoint, your pit stop in the resilience race.

After facing each setback, take a moment to reflect on your action plan. Did it work? Was it effective? Could it be improved? This reflection will give you valuable insights into your resilience strategy, helping you tweak and fine-tune your action plan for future setbacks.

Remember, your resilience plan is not set in stone. It's a living, evolving guide that grows with you. It's about learning from each setback, adapting your strategy, and building your resilience muscle.

Chapter 7

Fueling Your Dreams: The Power of Sleep and Nutrition for Teens

What are two things most teens don't get enough of but desperately need? If you read the chapter title and guessed quality sleep and proper nutrition, give yourself a pat on the back. You're spot on! Poor sleep and nutrition is like trying to ride a bike with a flat tire or drive a car with an empty fuel tank. If you're a typical teenager, you probably prefer to stay up late with friends, play video games, watch tv or scroll through reels while your eyes bug out of your head, instead of getting to bed early. All the while, you're probably snacking on something sugary sweet that's lacking in any real nutritional value. It's okay - you're normal. But let's talk about why sleep and nutrition are so important, and maybe you'll be motivated just a little bit to give your body a little more love now so you can reap the benefits at school, work, and in your future ahead.

Sleep: More Important Than You Think

Sleep Quality and Health

Like a Beethoven symphony, sleep has rhythms and cycles. And just as a symphony isn't merely about the number of notes it contains, sleep isn't just about the number of hours you clock in. While it is essential to get *enough* sleep (a teenager should get 8-10 hours of sleep a night), the *quality* of sleep is equally important.

You know the feeling when you wake up after a full night's sleep but still feel like a sloth stuck in slow motion? That's your body telling you that quality doesn't always equal quantity.

When you sleep, your body is hard at work, repairing cells, consolidating memories, and recharging your heart and cardiovascular system. It's like your body's version of housekeeping. When sleep quality is poor, this essential housekeeping suffers. Your immune system weakens, making you more susceptible to illnesses. Your mood swings like a pendulum, causing emotional roller coasters. Your risk of chronic conditions like obesity, diabetes, and heart disease increases. It's like running a marathon with weights strapped to your feet: you can do it, but it will take a toll.

Sleep Cycles and Brain Function

Each night, you cycle through different sleep stages- from light to deep sleep and finally, REM (Rapid Eye Movement) sleep. Each cycle is important and has many different roles to play.

Light sleep, also known as non-REM sleep, is a transitional phase between being awake and deep sleep. During light sleep, several critical processes occur. Your muscles start to relax, and it's normal to have some twitching or jerking movements. Your body temperature and awareness of external stimuli begin to decrease. Brain waves slow down, and dreaming may occur, but they're usually shorter and less vivid dreams than dreams during REM sleep. Light sleep plays a role in consolidating memories and processing information from the day. However, most of that is done during deep sleep. Light sleep does contribute to the body's overall restoration and rejuvenation, but most of this occurs during deeper cycles of sleep. Many teenagers (and adults, for that matter) spend most of their nights in light sleep, without enough time in deeper sleep cycles, and this is where sleep quality is lacking and true health suffers.

Deep sleep is like reaching the coziest, most relaxing part of your sleep journey. It's when your body and brain get a chance to do vital maintenance work. During deep sleep, your body releases growth hormone which is used to help your muscles and tissues grow and repair. If you've been active during the day, your body uses this time to rebuild what you've used up. Think of your brain as like a super busy office where people have been working and running around all day. During deep sleep, the cleaning crew comes in to clean up. Your brain organizes all the information gathered during the day, deciding what to keep and what to take out to the trash. This process helps you remember things better and learn new stuff. Deep sleep also plays a crucial role in managing your emotions. It enables you to process and understand your feelings so you can wake up refreshed, more balanced, and ready to take on a new day. You can still dream during deep sleep, but these dreams are often more logical and less wild than in the next stage of sleep. It's tough for someone to wake you up during deep sleep. You might be aware of loud noises, but you probably won't notice most sounds or things happening around you. Deep sleep is like the VIP of your sleep journey. It's where your body and mind do the most essential work so you can wake up feeling refreshed and ready to take on the world.

Next up is **REM sleep**. This is your brain's playtime. Your dreams are most vivid and wild during REM sleep. Your brain is incredibly active during this time. But even though your brain is buzzing with activity, your body stays mostly still. Your eyes move quickly in different directions (hence the name Rapid Eye Movement sleep), but the rest of your body is relaxed. During REM sleep, you also process emotions and experiences from your day. It helps you make sense of things that happened, and sometimes, it can even help you solve problems or understand your feelings better. Believe it or not, REM sleep is crucial for learning and memory. It helps you store and organize all the cool things you've learned and experienced during your day, making it easier for you to remember them later.

When your sleep cycles are disrupted, it's like your body and brain are trying to dance to a song with a skipping beat. They don't sync up properly, which can affect how you feel and function during the day. You can wake up feeling groggy, be more susceptible to mood swings, have trouble concentrating or remembering things, and you're likely to have low energy. Over time, regular sleep disruptions can lead to more severe health issues, like a weakened immune system, weight gain, and even an increased risk for certain diseases.

Sleep Environment and Hygiene

So, how can you ensure that your sleep is sufficient, sound, and restorative? The answer lies in your sleep environment and hygiene.

Your sleep **environment** includes your bedroom's light, noise, and temperature. Ideally, your bedroom should be dark, quiet, and cool. Consider using earplugs or a white noise machine if you can't control the noise (though less sound is always better) and eye shades or blackout curtains to block out light (it doesn't need to be pitch black, but there should be minimal light). If you need a nightlight, use a red light instead of a standard white light. Red light doesn't disrupt your brain, and you'll still be able to get a good night's sleep. When I transitioned my son from a regular night light to a red night light, suddenly, his sleep quantity and quality went from horrible to perfectly normal. It's worth the switch!

Sleep **hygiene** refers to habits that help you have quality sleep. This includes sticking to a sleep schedule, having a bedtime routine, avoiding caffeine and large meals close to bedtime, and turning off electronic devices an hour before bed. When you have a regular nighttime routine, your brain will anticipate what's coming next and start to prepare for a good night's sleep, even before your head hits the pillow.

You've probably heard about blue light, which is strongly emitted by the sun during the day. The devices we all use (phones, tv's, computers, etc) also emit intense blue light, which can severely disrupt our sleep cycles. You can mitigate some of the damaging effects of the light by either wearing blue light-blocking glasses in the evening, or by turning off your devices at least an hour before bed so your brain isn't constantly stimulated by the unnatural blue light. It's one way to help your brain get the best sleep possible.

Combined, a good sleep environment and proper sleep hygiene set the stage for quality sleep. They're your tickets to waking up refreshed, energized, and ready to tackle the day head-on. Quality sleep is arguably the most important thing to pay attention to if you want to feel good, look good, and go far, so don't take this lightly.

The Sleep vs. Stress Seesaw

The Effect of Stress on Sleep

Sometimes, you're lying in bed, eyes closed, ready to drift off into dreamland, but your mind has other plans. It's racing, running through an endless to-do list, replaying the day's events, or worrying about tomorrow's challenges. Sound familiar? It could be anxiety, or it could just be a racing mind, but to your body, it's all the same: it's stress.

Stress activates your body's fight or flight response, putting your body on high alert. Your heart rate speeds up, your muscles tense, and your thoughts race. It's like your body is preparing for a marathon when it should be gearing up for a good night's rest.

The result? Tossing and turning, a restless night, and poor sleep. Stress prevents quality sleep.

Effect of Sleep Deprivation on Stress Levels

Now, let's flip the script. Imagine you've pulled an all-nighter cramming for a test, or binge-watching your favorite show. The next day, you're cranky and jittery, and everything seems to get on your nerves. That's sleep deprivation at work.

Lack of sleep throws your brain and body off balance and raises stress hormones. It affects your mood, making you even *more* susceptible to stress. Even minor annoyances can seem like major problems, and coping with stress becomes an uphill battle. Plus, sleep deprivation can make you more prone to accidents and errors, adding to your stress levels. It's like a leaky faucet that keeps filling your stress bucket, drop by drop.

Sleep deprivation creates stress.

Strategies to Break the Cycle

So, how do you break this vicious sleep-stress cycle? It's like untangling a knot. You need to patiently work on loosening the tight spots and smoothing out the tangles, one at a time.

Start with stress management. Find healthy outlets for your stress, like physical activity, relaxation techniques, and hobbies. Talk to someone you trust about the things that worry or concern you. And don't forget to laugh! Laughter is a natural stress-buster, helping to lighten your mood and relax your body. Make sure your nutrition is on point, as that can significantly impact sleep, and as we'll talk about in just a bit, poor nutrition increases stress hormones as well.

Next, prioritize sleep. Remember what you just learned about sleep environment and sleep hygiene. Stick to a regular sleep schedule, even on weekends. Create a restful sleep environment free from distractions. Establish relaxing pre-sleep rituals, like reading a book, listening to soft music, or taking a warm bath.

Sleep and stress are closely intertwined, but you can untangle this complex knot with the right strategies. Take small but consistent steps towards better sleep and lower stress, and you'll improve both over time. And trust me, your body and mind will thank you for it.

Create Your Ideal Sleep Plan

Take out your notes or workbook (page 59), and let's do a little exercise to increase awareness of your current sleep habits. Reflect on your sleep quality, including your sleep environment and hygiene, and write down how you feel your sleep is right now. Then, take a look at where you think you can improve. Write out ways to improve, then pick one to work on for the next week or two. It might be going to bed at the same time each night, taking a warm bath to calm down, reading for 15 minutes, doing some meditation or journaling. Use some of the ideas given throughout this chapter if you're struggling to come up with some of your own. Remember, making small, doable changes one at a time is best - you don't need to overhaul your sleep all at once. Once you've mastered one idea, move on to the next.

The Teen's Guide to Nutrition

Good nutrition is essential for everyone, but it's especially crucial for teenagers, as this is a time of rapid growth and development. Your nutrition affects your physical growth, brain development, energy levels, and hormone balance. Good nutrition will help you stay at a healthy weight, help prevent illness and disease, and it can affect your mental health.

Of the many hats I wear, one is that of a certified nutrition coach, and I'm minorly obsessed with nutrition. So forgive me if I get a little excited about this topic! I want to teach you some basics so you understand why the quality of food you eat matters.

Understand Macronutrients and Micronutrients

At some point in school, you'll learn about macronutrients and micronutrients, but let's go over them now, though this won't be an in-depth lesson. Consider them the building blocks your body needs to function at its best.

Macronutrients are the big guys on the block. You need them in larger amounts, and they each have an important role to play. They come in three main types: carbohydrates, proteins, and fats. You need them all; please understand this. In our current world and culture, it's common to demonize one macronutrient or the other, but please don't give in to fad diet culture.

- Carbohydrates are your body's fuel, providing energy to every cell so it can function.

- Proteins are the body's building blocks, crucial for growth and repair.

- Fats are essential for cell integrity, absorption of vitamins, and hormone production.

Balance is the name of the game here.

Micronutrients, on the other hand, are the little guys. You need them in smaller amounts, but they play big roles. We're talking vitamins and minerals, each with specific jobs, from boosting your immune system to strengthening your bones.

Think of macronutrients and micronutrients as your body's dream team. They work together to keep you healthy, energized, and ready to rock your teen years like a boss. The goal is to eat macronutrients that are stuffed with as many micronutrients as possible, and to eat enough to fuel your growth, brain, and activity.

Importance of Hydration

Water plays a crucial role in nearly every bodily function. It's a key player in digestion, nutrient absorption, and even temperature regulation. You can think of water moving through your body like a flowing river: delivering nutrients to cells, picking up waste for disposal, and allowing it to flow out easily. You don't want the river to dry up and create stagnant puddles and dry ground.

But here's the catch - your body loses water through sweat, breathing, and even digestion. So, it needs a constant supply to keep the river running smoothly. Aim for at least 6-8 glasses daily, and more if you're active or it's a hot day. But since I know it's the thing these days to guzzle huge amounts of water, just a word: don't go crazy with plain water, especially if you're really active. If you drink too much plain water (especially filtered water that has had the minerals removed), you can deplete essential electrolytes, and *proper* hydration comes from keeping your electrolytes balanced within the cell. If you're especially active, I recommend drinking electrolytes every day. There are a lot of different electrolyte drinks you can use, and they're all fine, but to keep it super simple, you could add a pinch of sea salt to one of your glasses of water each day. Or at the very least, make sure to throw a little bit of salt on your food at dinner. (Salt isn't the only important electrolyte, but it's a good start.) This isn't something to obsess over; just keep in mind that too much of a good thing (drinking gallons of plain water) can indeed lead to not so good things.

A quick word on caffeine. Caffeine doesn't actually *create* energy inside your body. Instead, it blocks the receptors that make you feel tired and that are trying to tell you that your body needs either sleep or nutrition so it can keep working hard. So, if you feel more energized with caffeine in your system, your body is actually still tired; you're just not feeling it. Over time, your body will fight harder to get what it needs (sleep or better nutrition), so you'll feel more tired and need more caffeine to help you feel less tired; and the cycle continues. Plus, caffeine has a diuretic effect (that means it makes you pee), so it can actually dehydrate your body. A little caffeine each day is fine, but be aware that it's not creating real energy. And too much is damaging over time and will lead to dependency and possible burnout. What does create energy? Carbohydrates + oxygen + water, all working happily together within a cell.

Read and Understand Food Labels

In the words of my son's roommate, "Food is food." I get it - you're a hungry teen, and you probably don't really care where your food comes from. But take this opportunity to learn something new. Awareness... remember?

We're going to talk about food labels because I know there are a lot of gas station and grocery store food hunts that take place during high school. Preferably, you wouldn't be eating a lot of food that uses a food label, but I'm a mom - I understand that there's no avoiding it for teens. So imagine you're in a grocery store, staring at a shelf full of snack bars, and you're trying to pick the best option. That's where food labels come in handy. Food labels can be tricky, but I will help you know what to look for.

Start with the serving size. You might be surprised that the serving size is often much smaller than you think. You might think a whole bar is one serving, but sometimes they surprise you with one bar being two or three servings. It's worth looking at to know for sure.

Next, look at the calories. Calories aren't my favorite thing to focus on, but they give you an easy reference point for what you're about to consume. Active teen boys need about 2,600 to 3,200 calories daily, and active teen girls need about 2,200 to 2,400. So if one serving of your favorite chips is 900 calories for 3 chips, and you usually eat 37 chips at a time, you might want to reconsider those chips (that's obviously a big stretch, but there is some truth to it).

Now, check out the nutrients list. Remember our friends, the macronutrients and micronutrients? They're listed there, along with the amounts present in the food. Aim for foods high in fiber, vitamins, and minerals and lower in sodium, fats, and added sugars. Packaged foods usually contain excessive amounts of sodium, fats, and sugars.

Finally, take a peek at the ingredients list. Ingredients are listed in order of amount, from highest to lowest. So, if sugar is the first ingredient, you might want to reconsider your choice. Aim for foods that come as close to nature as possible, and try to keep the chemicals and frankenfoods out of your body as much as you can.

While we're at it, let's talk about sugar and fat here for just a minute, as these are two of the most demonized foods.

Is sugar bad? Not really. Sugar turns to glucose inside your body, and glucose is used by every cell to function and produce energy. When you eat any carbohydrate (fruits, vegetables, grains, beans, pure table sugar), it all turns to glucose inside your body. What makes sugar "bad" is that there are huge amounts of it in so many foods and it lacks micronutrients - the vitamins and minerals your body needs. So eating a lot of "sugar" fills your belly but doesn't give your body any real nutrition. If you crave sugar, your body is craving energy through proper nutrition. Try eating a whole bunch of fruit and see if that does the trick. Fruit will provide your body with the glucose it craves, but it will also give you a huge boost of vitamins, minerals, and fiber. Fruit also has its own sugar, called fructose, which is hugely beneficial when combined with glucose. "Sugar cravings" are often a result of not eating enough, especially enough nutrient-dense foods. When your body feels like it doesn't have the fuel it needs to perform the tasks required of it, it will crave the quickest form of energy it knows of, and usually, that's sugary candy. If you struggle with a sweet tooth or night binging, try eating more nutrient-dense foods throughout the day and see what happens.

As a side note, *any* food craving is your body trying to tell you something. Instead of "fighting" the craving, give your body the most nutrient-dense version of what it's craving, and I promise you'll be healthier for it and will experience fewer cravings over time.

How about fat? Is fat bad? Not really. You need natural fats to develop hormones, absorb certain micronutrients, and hold your cells together. Where we go wrong with fats is that 1: they're easy to get too much of, 2: fats go rancid quickly and change their chemical makeup so your body doesn't process it well, and 3: fat is where toxins are stored, so you have to be careful with some animal fats, as you can be eating toxins along with the fat. Gross. This is why packaged foods aren't always a great option - they typically have rancid or chemically changed fats and usually way more than our body needs. Eating natural fats found in foods like dairy, grass-fed steak, and avocado is perfectly fine. You might even be surprised to know there are small amounts of fat in many fruits and vegetables. Our bodies need fat, just not a lot of it, so go easy on the added butter, cooking oils, and anything prepackaged with a good amount of fat in it.

What about fast food? There are definitely some fast food places that are okay, but others that should probably be avoided altogether. You can usually find the food-label equivalent for fast foods on the company's website. The key is being aware of the type of ingredients a company uses. No matter where it comes from, if it's fried, it will most definitely have rancid oils that your body will struggle to process. Another red flag is if it doesn't go bad after sitting on the counter for 2 days, it's full of chemical preservatives that your body will store in your fat cells in order to keep you safe. Chemical preservatives are no bueno, and some fast food companies are notorious for using a ton of preservatives. Do some research into what ingredients you're ingesting, and do your best to avoid things your body won't recognize as real food.

Eating in the Real World

Hopefully, you now have a better idea of why nutrition is important and what good nutrition can do for your body. I urge you to be smart about your nutrition - don't try to be perfect, and don't take it for granted, either. If you want to look good and feel good, you can do that by eating average amounts of food as well as having treats every once in a while. If you're active, you'll need more food; if you're sedentary, you'll need less than active kids - it's that simple. Food is an integral part of your overall health and wellness, but it's not the only part. If you struggle with eating too little or overeating, I urge you to talk to an adult who can help you. If you are confused by all the diet information out there, I encourage you to stand out by being "anti-diet." Go back to basic biology and know that eating natural, whole foods of all kinds is a great way to take care of your body. Still, it's also okay to live in the real world and splurge on treats here and there. Listen to your body, eat when you're hungry, stop when you're full, and don't listen if others tell you that you can or can't eat certain macronutrients (unless, of course, you have a diagnosed allergy or sensitivity). Focus on eating a wide range of micronutrient-dense foods, so your organs, muscles, and bones have everything they need to grow, repair, and function properly.

Take a Look at Your Current Nutrition Habits

Once again, take out your notes or workbook (page 63), and let's do another exercise to increase awareness about your current nutrition habits. Write down what you typically eat in a day. Maybe use today as your example. Don't judge yourself by feeling extra good or bad because you ate this or that. Just write out the facts of what you eat. Now, note how much of your diet is close to nature. How many fruits? How many vegetables and leafy greens? Despite what culture tells us, vegetables aren't "better" than fruit - fruits are equally amazing and full of incredible nutrition. Adding fruit is a great place to start improving your nutrition because it tastes fantastic and is easy to eat. Of course, eat those veggies too! What about grains? Legumes (beans)? Protein from things like meat and dairy? Are you getting any of that in? If you're mainly eating packaged foods, that's okay! This is your starting place.

Write down one or two ways to get a few more nutrients in your day. It might be as simple as eating a banana with your lunch. If you're eating many foods you know aren't great for your body, I don't recommend cutting foods out initially. I'd rather you *add* nutritious foods and continue to do so until the less nutritious foods are eventually squeezed out of your diet. If you would rather make the jump to remove certain foods, go ahead and try it for a day or two and see what happens. If you're successful, keep going for another day or two. Work on adding nutrient-dense foods until your day is filled with foods that make you AND your body happy.

Changing our food habits is hard to do on our own, especially when you're not the one purchasing the food for your family. Talk with your parents about your goals and ways you can work together to make these small changes over time.

Part 2: Practical and Technical Life Skills

In Part 2 of this book, you'll learn more practical and technical life skills, like managing time and money, meal planning, and cleaning. We'll also talk about using your time online and how to protect yourself in the online world. This section will give you the skills you need to one day be successful living on your own. Learning and practicing these skills now will help you have a firm handle on them when that time comes.

Chapter 8

The Balancing Act: Time Management

You're at a large amusement park, excited to try all the thrilling rides, gobble up all the delicious food, and play all the games - maybe even win a giant stuffed bear. But there's one little catch - there's enough to keep you busy for three days, but you're only there for a single day. Suddenly, you're left with too much to do but too little time. Welcome to the 24-hour day, the grand amusement park of life. It's packed with rides named school, homework, sports, chores, sleep, and, oh, don't forget the fun-house of social life. So, how do you make the most of this 24-hour ticket without missing out on the fun or ending up exhausted? You need a solid plan of action.

Make the Most of 24 Hours

We all get the same 24 hours, but what sets achievers apart is how they use that time. It's not about having more time; it's about making the most of your time, and that takes understanding what needs to happen, prioritizing, planning, discipline, and commitment. That sounds like a lot. Some people naturally use their time wisely, while others struggle. As someone who struggles, I promise you that this skill can be learned, practiced, and honed. With a solid plan, you can ride all those rides, eat all the food, and win all the prizes with time to spare.

Understand Time Perception

Have you ever experienced the phenomenon where time seems to slip away effortlessly while binge-watching your favorite show: five hours passing in what feels like mere moments? Conversely, sitting through a tedious lecture can make every minute drag on endlessly as if time has come to a standstill. This contrast in perception, where the same 60 seconds or 60 minutes can feel drastically different depending on the activity, highlights the intriguing ways our minds can play tricks on us.

The way we perceive time can be as unpredictable as a rollercoaster ride. It's all about the ebb and flow of attention, emotions, and the amount of things we want to squeeze into our day. When you're focused on something that you enjoy or find interesting (like binge-watching your favorite series or playing video games), time seems to fly. On the other hand, when you're stuck in a situation that's boring, uncomfortable, or stressful (like that never-ending math class), each minute seems to crawl by.

Understanding time perception will help you better use your time by letting you know when you may not be using your time wisely or when you need to focus and increase patience to get through something important. Bringing awareness to the issue: if you know that every time you start to scroll reels, 3 hours suddenly go by, you can implement a plan to avoid wasting that precious time.

Factors Affecting Time Management

Several factors can thwart even our best efforts to manage our time wisely.

- First up, we've got **distractions**. They're like those annoying pop-up ads that interrupt your online game. Whether it's the constant buzz of your phone with social media notifications or that tempting TV show playing in the background, distractions can slice and dice your time like a ninja.

Minimize distractions by creating a focused environment. Clear away clutter, turn off notifications on your devices, and find a quiet space where you can concentrate. Use website blockers if necessary, and let those around you know when you need uninterrupted focus. Developing a disciplined routine and staying mindful of your surroundings can help you maintain concentration and accomplish tasks efficiently.

- Next on the list is **procrastination**, the sneaky thief of time. It's that comfy couch that lures you into lounging just when you're about to start your homework, or that easier task that you decide to complete instead of hitting the harder, more important task. Procrastination is often a sign that something feels too overwhelming or just isn't exciting enough for you to be motivated by it. Sometimes, you might procrastinate something because it feels scary or like you will fail if you try, and it's easier to just not try. Overcoming procrastination can be challenging, but with the right strategies, it's entirely possible.

One of my favorite ways to overcome procrastination is by breaking larger or scary tasks into smaller, more manageable ones. Large tasks can feel much more overwhelming, and sometimes, our brain just wants to avoid the task altogether. So breaking a large task down into smaller ones can be a great strategy.

For instance, if I want my son to clean his disaster of a room, it'll never actually happen because it's too overwhelming for him. But if I tell him to start with just the books scattered around his room, he's more willing to get that smaller task done right away. A similar method is to clean in small sections, or I might tell him to work on his room for 5 minutes and get done whatever he can in that time. Breaking the task into small pieces or setting a timer for 5-10 minutes is a great way to get started on something that feels daunting or boring.

Creating a to-do list can also be helpful when trying to overcome procrastination. Sometimes, you just don't know where to start. Think through the project, create small steps, and get to work on the first step.

- Next up on factors affecting our time management is being **over-scheduled**. This can be a big problem for teenagers. When my oldest son was in high school, he thought taking AP classes most of his day was a great idea. That looks great on paper, right? I love that he was thinking ahead for college, but he was way too overscheduled. He had too much homework and still had extracurricular activities he wanted to participate in. It started to really stress him out and break him down. Sometimes, by no fault of your own, you're doing your best to do *all* the things, and even if you don't struggle with procrastination or distractions - you just have too much to do. We'll talk more about this later, but I know this can be a big problem for some teens.

- Lastly, **poor planning** can ruin all your well-intended time management plans. It's like going on a road trip without GPS. You end up wandering aimlessly, wasting time, and probably missing out on the best spots. Coming up soon, we will talk about different strategies to lay out a workable plan so you can manage your time the best way possible.

Analyze Your 24 Hours

It's time to pull out those notes or workbook (page 67) so we can bring some awareness to your own time management struggles or successes. Take a minute to think through your typical day. Jot down activities you find yourself getting lost in and spending too much time on. Is the time you spend on those activities helping you become the person you want to be, or are they keeping you from getting things done that are more, or equally important? (If you get lost in doing research, I feel you.) Sometimes, it's good things we're losing our time on (like researching cool stuff), but sometimes, those good things keep you from getting other good things done.

Now, write down everything you want or need to be doing but can't seem to get done. Think about why you might not be able to get those things done.

- Do you tend to procrastinate? If yes, dig deeper and consider *why* you're prone to procrastination. Is it because tasks feel too big? Too hard? Too scary?

- What about distractions? Do you struggle with homework because your little sister is watching TV in the other room?

- Or maybe you just have too many good things you're trying to do.

This activity can be challenging because sometimes we don't want to admit we need to change. But step away from emotions here and just take this opportunity to identify exactly how the time in your day is being spent, and if you're unable to get everything done that you feel is important, identify what is happening that is preventing you from doing those things. You may have to dig deep here and really think through what's going on. Write it out to bring awareness to it - you're not trying to fix anything just yet. We'll talk strategies next.

Prioritize Like a Boss

Imagine your day as a backpack. You can only fit a certain number of things inside it, right? Time works the same way. You have 24 hours in a day, and just like your backpack has limited space, your time is limited, too. Time prioritization is like deciding what to put in your backpack first because some things are more important than others.

When you prioritize your time, you decide what activities or tasks are most important to you and your goals. For example, finishing your homework might be a high priority because it helps you do well in school. Spending time with your family or friends could also be a priority because it makes you happy and strengthens your relationships.

To prioritize your time effectively, you need to figure out what matters most to you. This means understanding your goals, whether related to school, hobbies, sports, or personal development. Once you know your goals, you can decide which activities help you reach them.

Think of it like this: If you want to improve at playing the guitar, practicing regularly becomes a high-priority activity because it helps you achieve your goal. Watching TV, on the other hand, might be fun, but it's a lower-priority activity because it doesn't directly contribute to your goal of improving your guitar skills.

Time prioritization is about making conscious choices. It's about putting the most important tasks and activities into your day first, just like you'd put the most important stuff in your backpack first. By doing this, you make sure you're using your time wisely and working toward the things that matter most to you.

Following are several methods of task prioritization that you can try. Decide which sounds most doable to you and try it out for a week. If it doesn't help keep you on task, try a different one.

The Eisenhower Matrix

This a cool tool named after the 34th U.S. President, Dwight D. Eisenhower. This handy matrix is like a sorting hat for your tasks, dividing them into four categories: Do First, Decide / Schedule, Delegate, and Delete or Delay. Let's break it down.

The '**Do First**' category is for tasks that are both important and urgent. They're the red flashing lights that need immediate attention. This could be studying for a test or finishing a project due tomorrow.

Next, we have the '**Decide When To Do or Schedule**' category. These are important but not urgent tasks and typically apply to longer-term tasks requiring planning or decision-making. This could be planning your study schedule for the next week or researching colleges you want to apply to. Plan a specific date to complete these tasks; get them on your calendar.

Then comes the '**Delegate**' category. Delegating means giving the task to someone else who is more able to complete it. These tasks may be important but they're not urgent or they don't contribute much to your long-term goals. This could be if someone asks you for a favor that really makes your day difficult, or a club meeting you could attend virtually instead of in person. Ask yourself: "can someone else do this, or can the task be simplified?"

Finally, the '**Delete or Delay**' category. These tasks are neither important nor urgent. This could be that video game marathon or the endless social media scrolling. Many of these may be tasks or time sucks that you should probably just cut out of your life completely. If it's something that feels important to you, but in the big scheme of life you know it's not important, then delay the task until everything else you need to do is done.

Using the Eisenhower Matrix, you can sort your tasks based on their urgency and importance, helping you focus on what truly matters. When you have so many things you need and want to do but are unsure where to start, using this tool can be helpful.

The ABCDE Method

This is a similar technique - the ABCDE Method. It's like a grading system for your tasks, helping you decide which ones deserve an 'A' and which can slide down to a 'D' or 'E.'

'A' tasks are your biggies, the ones that have serious potential consequences. These tasks align with your long-term goals and values like studying for the big test or completing homework.

'B' tasks are important but may not have an immediate deadline. Planning for a school project or working on a personal project at home are examples of B tasks.

'C' tasks are nice to do but don't have significant consequences if they don't get done. They're things like organizing your room or checking social media.

'D' tasks can be delegated. They're important enough to be done, but not necessarily by you.

'E' tasks can be eliminated. They're the time-wasters, the tasks that don't contribute to your goals or values and should probably be eliminated entirely.

By grading your tasks using the ABCDE Method, you can decide which tasks deserve your time and energy and which ones don't. You can also assign tasks a number within each category. For example, if you have five tasks assigned as A priority, you can also assign each of those tasks a number (A1, A2, A3, etc) to further prioritize them.

The Pareto Principle

Finally, let's explore the Pareto Principle, also known as the 80/20 rule. It's like the golden productivity ratio, stating that roughly 80% of your results come from 20% of your efforts.

For example:

- You might notice that 80% of your exam grades come from studying the most critical 20% of the topics

- You might wear 20% of your clothes 80% of the time

- In a video game, you might find that 80% of your achievements come from mastering 20% of the skills

Regarding time management, this means that a small number of tasks (the 20%) will lead to the majority of your achievements (the 80%). Your job is to identify these high-value tasks that give you the biggest bang for your buck and give them the attention they deserve.

Make a list of tasks you think are in the 20% for you; those tasks that will lead you to achieve 80% of your goals (homework, football or piano practice, etc.). Focus on getting these tasks accomplished first, then you can use your extra time on the other things you'd like to add to your day.

***

Try these methods out for size to see which one is a good fit in your life. Remember, it's not about doing more but about doing what matters. There's space in the workbook (starting on page 71) for you to try out each of these methods, or just make a note on your phone or on paper with your list of priorities.

The Art of Saying No

Learning to say no is a crucial skill for mastering time management. As adolescents, you're often pulled in multiple directions – school, extracurricular activities, social events, and family obligations. Saying yes to everything might seem like a friendly thing, but it can quickly lead to being overwhelmed and burned out. By learning to say no, you gain the power to prioritize your commitments and focus on what truly matters.

Saying no isn't about being rude; it's about setting boundaries and ensuring that your activities align with your goals and well-being. It empowers you to manage your time effectively, allowing you to dedicate ample energy to the tasks and activities that genuinely contribute to your personal growth, academic success, and overall happiness. Mastering this skill helps you avoid spreading yourself too thin. It fosters a sense of control, enabling you to make the most out of your teenage years and set a strong foundation for your future.

Indeed, you don't want to be someone who says no to *everything*. The idea is to find a balance so you can still be a dependable person who is willing to help others out, but you're not getting steamrolled into taking on tasks that stress you and you don't have time for. It's important to be friendly and willing to help and serve others, but not at the expense of your sanity. If you're feeling too overwhelmed and a request just loads on stress, learning to say no is an important skill.

Identify Time Thieves

We touched on time thieves when we talked about time perception, but we will dig a little deeper now. Time thieves come in all shapes and sizes. Maybe it's that chatty friend who keeps you on the phone for hours talking or texting, or that addictive video game, or social media. Perhaps it's hanging around after school for too long chatting with friends, or turning on YouTube or Netflix as soon as you get home. It could be that you're a perfectionist, so you spend too much extra time making sure a project is just so. Or maybe it's having to clean up a room that never should have gotten so messy in the first place, or being unable to concentrate because of the room's chaos. Maybe a lack of planning leads you to do and redo things that could have been done more efficiently if planned out better.

Consider what time thieves you're dealing with and write them down (page 79 in the workbook). Learn to say "no" to time thieves by developing strategies to overcome them. Strategies could include using the prioritizing skills you just learned above, setting boundaries, improving your planning and scheduling methods (we'll talk about both of those next), or coming up with alternative activities.

Set Boundaries

Imagine your time as a beautiful garden. Boundaries are like the fence around this garden, protecting it from intruders and keeping it safe and flourishing.

Setting boundaries is defining your time limits and sticking to them. It's about deciding what you're willing to spend your time on and what you're not. It's about making conscious choices that align with your priorities and values and saying no to things that don't.

Boundaries not only protect your time, they also boost your self-esteem, reduce stress, and improve your relationships. Triple win! By setting clear boundaries, you're asserting your right to control your time, preventing burnout, and teaching others to respect your time. Your time is precious, so guard it fiercely, invest it wisely, and cherish it deeply. Decide what your boundaries need to be, and don't be afraid to communicate that to others.

Maybe you decide you can only talk with friends for 10 minutes after school, or you put your phone away during homework time, or you can only watch YouTube on a particular day of the week. Think of some boundaries that will effectively help you use your time more wisely and write them down (page 81 in the workbook).

Assertive Communication

As you're expressing your time boundaries to people, you can use what's called assertive communication. Assertive communication is about expressing your needs and wants clearly and confidently without being aggressive or passive. It's about standing up for your time rights without trampling over others' rights. It's about saying "no" in a way that respects both your time and the other person's feelings. Using assertive communication properly will help you overcome those time thieves and set proper boundaries.

So, how do you do it? Start with "I" statements. For example, instead of saying, "You're always wasting my time with your endless chatter," try saying, "I need to focus on my homework right now. Can we chat later?" or "I've decided that I have to keep my phone turned off during homework, so I may not respond to you until after dinner time." It's less accusatory, more respectful, and gets the point across without sparking a conflict.

When using assertive communication, remember all those skills you learned about communicating in Chapters 2 and 3. Think of your body language, and don't forget to practice active listening. Being assertive doesn't have to feel mean, but it ensures that your opinions and feelings are acknowledged and respected.

It may be helpful to write out some "I statements" that you can use to make sure your friends know your time boundaries. Take a minute now to write a few down so you're prepared when the time comes to talk to your friends and set those boundaries (page 83 in the workbook). Keep in mind that you can use "I" statements to express yourself in any situation, not just when it comes to managing your time.

Your Personal Time Management Plan

We will put it all together now and create your perfect week – one that works for you in the real world. This is your time management plan that will help you prioritize and weed out the time thieves, help you get everything done that you need to, and hopefully leave you with some time to do all those fun extra things, too.

Time Blocking Technique

Time Blocking is a simple and powerful technique to organize your time around your priorities. Work through the following steps, and you'll have a well-planned way to manage your time. There's a place to do this in the workbook (page 85), or doing it digitally on a spreadsheet is also a simple tool.

Step 1: **List Your Tasks**

Identify everything you need to accomplish during the week. This includes homework, studying, extracurricular activities, chores, social time, exercise, and relaxation. Write down everything you need to do.

Step 2: **Prioritize Your Tasks**

Determine which tasks are most important and time-sensitive. For instance, homework and studying might be top priorities during the weekdays. Social activities and hobbies can be planned around these priorities. This is a great time to use the ABCDE method to prioritize, but if you prefer one of the other methods, use that.

Step 3: **Allocate Specific Time Blocks**

Divide your day into blocks of time. For example, use hours or half-hours as your blocks, listed from when you wake up to when you go to bed. Assign specific tasks to each block. Be realistic about the time each task will take. Here are some examples of tasks to put into your hour or half-hour blocks:

- Morning routine: Allocate time for waking up, getting ready, and having breakfast.

- School: Block out the hours you're in school. Include travel time if you walk, bike, or take the bus.

- Homework/Studying: Assign specific blocks for homework and studying. Break larger tasks into smaller tasks if they don't fit into one block.

- Extracurricular activities: Include time for clubs, sports, music lessons, or any other activities you participate in.

- A job: If you have a job, block out the time you're scheduled to work. Be sure to include travel time.

- Chores: Allocate time for chores like cleaning your room, doing dishes, or helping with family tasks.

- Social time: Plan time to hang out with friends, chat online, or play games.

- Exercise: Dedicate time for physical activity, even if it's just a short workout or a walk around the neighborhood.

- Relaxation: Schedule downtime for hobbies, reading, watching TV, or relaxing. This time is essential for your mental well-being.

- Self-care: Remember to include time for self-care activities like getting enough sleep and preparing and/or eating healthy meals. Taking care of yourself helps you stay focused and energized.

Step 4: **Be Flexible**

Life is unpredictable. Be prepared to adjust your schedule when unexpected events occur. It's okay to rearrange your blocks as long as you ensure that essential tasks are still completed.

Step 5: **Use Technology** if it's helpful

Consider using digital tools or apps designed for scheduling and time management. These tools can send reminders and help you stay organized, especially if you have a lot on your plate.

Step 6: **Review and Adjust**

At the end of each week, assess how well you stuck to your schedule. Identify what worked and what didn't. Adjust your schedule for the next week based on this evaluation.

By following these steps and being consistent, you can create a time-blocking schedule that helps you manage your tasks efficiently while ensuring you have time for your interests and relaxation. If you find you have more tasks to do than time to do them, this is where you need to use your prioritization skills and learn to say no. Sometimes, it's not that we can't do something at all; it's that we can't do it right now.

Chapter 9

Living In An Online World

We all spend a lot of our time online these days. It can be necessary, but it's also just fun and entertaining. Since we spend so much time online, it's important to learn some valuable skills to do so safely and responsibly.

Understand Your Digital Footprint

The Tracks We Leave Behind

Imagine you're walking on the moon, leaving footprints in the moon sand as you walk along. With each step, you leave a mark, a trace of where you've been. Sometimes, the online world can feel like you're on the moon, right? Well, those same footprints happen in the virtual world. Every click, every post, every search leaves a mark - a digital footprint. And just like your footprints in the moon sand can be seen by anyone else who walks on the moon (stay with me here), your digital footprints can be seen, and sometimes even tracked, by others online.

Whenever you browse the web, post a photo on Instagram, or purchase online, you leave a trail of digital breadcrumbs. It's like your shadow in the digital world, following you wherever you go. This trail, or digital footprint, is a record of your online activity. It's a snapshot of who you are, what you do, and what you like.

Think about it. When you log into Facebook, you might see ads for that cool new video game you searched for yesterday. Or when you watch a video on YouTube, it suggests more videos based on what you've watched before. These are examples of how your digital footprint is used to tailor your online experience.

The Long-Term Effects of Your Digital Footprint

Now, let's consider a future scenario. Imagine you're applying for a job or a college scholarship. The recruiter or admissions officer decides to do a quick Google search of your name. What will they find? Will it be a well-manicured digital portrait that showcases your strengths, interests, and achievements? Or will it be a jumble of embarrassing photos, reckless comments, or questionable content?

Your digital footprint can have long-term effects. It can influence job opportunities, college admissions, and even personal relationships. It can either open doors or close them. It's like the digital equivalent of a first impression, and we all know how much first impressions matter.

The Importance of Being Aware

So, what can you do about it? Well, here's that A-word again. Awareness. Be mindful of the digital footprints you're leaving. Before you post that photo, send that tweet, or make that comment, pause and think. Ask yourself, "Would I be okay with this being online forever?" Because once something is online, it can be hard to erase completely.

Being aware of your digital footprint is not just about being careful; it's also about being conscious. It's about understanding the impact of your online actions. It's about making informed choices that align with your values, goals, and the digital image you want to project.

How Conscious Are You of Your Digital Footprint?

Let's put your awareness to the test with a quick quiz. You can answer to yourself, write it down, or find the quiz in your notebook (page 89) to answer there.

1. Do you regularly check your social media privacy settings?

2. Before posting something online, do you consider its potential impact on your digital footprint?

3. Have you ever Googled yourself to see what information is available about you online?

4. Do you think about how your online behavior today might affect future opportunities?

You're on the right track if you answered 'yes' to most of these questions. If not, don't worry. Awareness is the first step, and you've already taken that by reading this chapter. Keep going, and remember, every click, every post, every search matters. So, tread carefully in the digital moon sands. Your future self will thank you for it.

Manage Your Digital Footprint

Schedule Regular Online Clean-ups

Just as you'd clean up after a hike, leaving the trail as pristine as you found it, cleaning up your digital trail regularly is a good idea. This means checking what information about you is available online. Google yourself and see what comes up. You might be surprised by how much you can find!

Delete or untag yourself from any old, inappropriate, or unnecessary posts or photos. Check your privacy settings on social media platforms, ensuring only the right people have access to your posts.

Shape Your Digital Shadow

Your online behavior doesn't just leave footprints; it casts a digital shadow, a silhouette that reflects who you are and how you behave online. This shadow can shape people's perception of you for better or worse. So, it's in your best interest to shape it positively.

Think about your personal brand and what you want people to think when they see your digital shadow. Maybe you want to be seen as creative, knowledgeable, or socially conscious. Then, align your online behavior with this image. Share posts and articles that reflect your interests and values. Engage with online communities that align with your personal brand.

Remember, your digital footprint and shadow are not just about now. They're echoes of your past and whispers of your future. They're a record of where you've been and a hint at where you're going. So, manage them wisely, with thoughtfulness and intention.

Protect Your Online Privacy

In the digital realm, privacy is like an invisible shield protecting your personal information from prying eyes. It's the seal that keeps your private life private, the lock that keeps your secrets safe. But just like any shield, it requires maintenance and vigilance to stay strong and effective.

The Password Paradox: Simplicity vs. Security

Passwords are like keys to your online home. The stronger they are, the harder it is for intruders to break in. However, the challenge lies in creating passwords that are complex enough so hackers can't figure them out but easy enough for you to remember. There's a good solution - password managers.

Think of password managers as a secure vault where all your passwords are stored. You only need to remember one master password to access the vault; the password manager takes care of the rest. It can generate strong, unique passwords for your online accounts and auto-fill them when needed.

There are several reliable password managers available, such as LastPass or Dashlane. They help create uncrackable passwords and save you the headache of remembering them all. Have a parent help you set one up.

App Permissions: The Fine Print of Digital Freedom

In the app-filled universe of our smartphones, every app is like a visitor requesting entry into your online home. And just like you wouldn't let a visitor roam freely around your house without knowing their purpose, you shouldn't grant permissions to apps without understanding why they need them.

When you install an app, it might ask for permission to access certain features or data on your device, like your camera, contacts, or location. But before you click accept, always ask yourself, "Does this app really need this permission to function properly?"

For example, a photo editing app might need access to your photos, but does it really need to know your location? Probably not. Be mindful of the permissions you grant, and don't hesitate to say 'no' when something doesn't feel right. It's like setting boundaries for the visitors to your online home, ensuring they respect your space and privacy.

Know Your Rights in the Digital World

In the realm of the internet, knowledge truly is power. Awareness of your digital information rights is crucial in managing your digital footprint. In an era where data is the new gold, it's essential to know who can access your data, how it can be used, and what control you have over it.

Many countries have established laws to protect individuals' data privacy. For example, the General Data Protection Regulation (GDPR) in the European Union gives individuals the right to access their personal data, correct inaccuracies, and even have their data erased in certain circumstances. The United States doesn't have a Federal law in place to match the GDPR, however, many individual states have their own laws that serve as equivalents. It's a good idea to know what laws are in place where you live to protect your privacy.

Review the privacy policies and terms of service of the websites and apps you use. While they may seem long and filled with complicated legal jargon, they contain important information about how your data is collected, stored, and used.

Digital Detox: Unplug for a Healthier You

You've gone to the world's most incredible party. The music's thumping, people are laughing, chatting, dancing. It's fun, right? But what if the party never ends? The constant noise and endless socializing could be overwhelming, even exhausting. That's what our brains can sometimes feel like when we spend all our time staring at screens. It's like a never-ending party. And just like you'd need a breather from a real party, your brain needs a break from the digital one, too. For the sake of good health, you might want to consider doing a little digital detox every once in a while to ensure you're staying grounded in the real world and to give your eyes and brain a break.

The Balance: Mindful Tech Usage

Going on a digital detox doesn't mean you have to renounce all technology and move to a remote cabin in the woods. It's not about cutting off but cutting down and being mindful of your usage. There are so many good things online, but also so many things that can be an absolute time suck. It's important to be mindful of the time you're spending looking at your phone or at any screen. If you struggle to put your phone away for any amount of time, scheduling breaks is a good idea. Devices are powerful these days and can be so wonderful, but they can also get in the way of important relationships or keep us from fulfilling our goals.

Consider this. You're at a lunch date with a friend. The food's delicious, the conversation's flowing, and then your phone buzzes. Do you check it, letting the digital world intrude into the real one? Or do you ignore it, choosing to stay fully present in the moment? Mindful tech usage is about making conscious choices about how you'll use technology in various situations instead of being driven by digital impulses.

Here are some ways you can be mindful of your technology usage:

- Be selective about the content you consume online. Choose educational and positive material over mindless scrolling.

- When spending time with friends or family, put your devices away so you can be fully engaged with others.

- Avoid multitasking while using technology.

- Establish specific time limits for screen use, including social media, gaming, and other digital activities.

- Designate tech-free zones, like the dinner table, the bathroom, or the bedroom (especially before bed).

It's easy to spend all your outside school time using technology, whether for important tasks like school work or leisure time. Be mindful of the time you use and set limits for yourself.

Offline Activities: The Hidden Gems

I know it can feel very difficult to spend time outside of school without your phone. So, what do you do when you unplug from the digital world? Well, the offline world is brimming with hidden gems waiting to be discovered. Remember that book gathering dust on your shelf? Or the guitar you've been meaning to learn to play? Or the park you've been planning to visit?

Engaging in offline activities not only gives your mind a much-needed break from screens, but it also contributes to your overall well-being. It's like stepping out of the virtual party into a quiet garden. You can hear the birds chirping, feel the sun on your face, and smell the fresh flowers. It's peaceful, grounding, and incredibly refreshing.

That's all a digital detox needs to be. Unplug to recharge, disconnect to reconnect, and turn off to tune in. It can feel very difficult at first, but the more you allow yourself to spend time without your phone, the more you'll discover how great it feels. So, take a deep breath, step away from the screen, and enter the vibrant, sensory world outside. You might be surprised by the magic you find there.

Chapter 10

Show Me the Money

M oney. One minute, you have it; the next minute, you have an armful of junk food and soda and empty pockets. It's time to take control of your cash flow, set yourself up for financial success, and become a money management pro. After all, it's great to buy all those little things now, but wouldn't it be better to eventually buy a car, a house, travel, or have money to take out and impress the girl or boy of your dreams? Having the ability to do those things takes discipline and some planning, but you don't have to give up every movie trip with your friends or every soda run to make it happen. You just have to figure out how to find a workable balance so you can enjoy life now *and* later. You need to prepare yourself a budget.

Here's a personal story. My sister is seven years older than I am. When I graduated high school, at 17 years old, she was almost 24 and finishing college. She and some of her friends were planning a backpacking trip through Europe, and I wanted nothing more than to go with them. I saved up as much as I could and paid for my trip entirely while she borrowed the money from our grandma to go. Granted, she was in college and had many more living expenses than I had since I was still living at home then. However, while we were roaming Europe, I carefully rationed my money to ensure I had enough to last the 9-week trip. That meant there were places I chose not to go and food I decided not to eat - things like that. She wasn't as careful, and guess what? She ran out of money when we still had 3 weeks left of our trip. We had to end our trip by staying at a family friend's house in England for those last 3 weeks. The only reason we didn't fly home early is because that cost more money! Ha! My sister is great! But even she admits she wasn't the greatest at budgeting back then.

It's not that I made a ton of money at the time and could go to Europe without significant planning. I knew what I wanted, and I made a plan to get it. It doesn't matter what your income is - if you're smart about budgeting, the world will open up to you, and you'll be able to do whatever you put your mind to. So what is it that *you* want to do?

Checking and Savings Basics

Let's start with the basics. As a kid, you probably mainly dealt with cash. Cash is easy because you can see it, and once it's gone, you know you can't spend any more money. As a teenager, you'll want to move on from just using cash to now dealing with a bank so you have a solid knowledge base of how banking works before you're out of the house and living on your own. You can have your parents help you open checking and savings accounts at their bank, which I recommend doing by the time you're 15 or 16 years old or when you have a job that pays you regularly. Banks have different requirements, so you'll have to check with your bank to see what they are as far as age or parental co-signing requirements.

Once you have a checking account, I recommend getting a debit card. A debit card looks just like a credit card, but it takes money directly out of your checking account when you use it. This is high-level stuff here! If you don't know how much money you have, you could easily overspend and be left with an empty bank account, plus fees, because banks don't like you to spend more money than you have. So you have to be *very* careful about using a debit card, and always be sure you're tracking your money closely.

Don't worry! This chapter will set you up for success so you can manage your money like a boss.

Income vs. Expenses

Simply put: income is the money you make; expenses are what you spend your money on. Your income will change with time, but consider how you're earning money right now. Do you have a job? Earn allowance? Or maybe you get birthday or Christmas money. No matter how you're earning money and no matter how much money you have at any given time, what you always need to remember is to keep your expenses *lower* than your income. In simple terms, never spend more money than you make.

We're not going to talk much more about income, except that you need to keep close track of exactly how much money you have coming in so you always know how much money you have to spend (or save - wink).

Needs vs. Wants

Let's play 'Would You Rather.' Would you rather have the latest smartphone or a roof over your head? Would you rather grab a burger at a fancy restaurant or fill up your car's gas tank? Those are clear choices, right? Certain things are more important than others. In the world of budgeting, we call these 'needs' and 'wants.' Simple enough, eh?

Needs are the essentials, the non-negotiables, the things you can't do without. Needs include expenses like rent, groceries, utilities, and transportation. Luckily, for most teenagers, you have fewer personal expenses that are considered needs. But as you get into college and beyond, suddenly, those expenses come out of nowhere, and you find yourself responsible for much more than you used to. So, knowing how to plan and prepare for those expenses now is a pivotal skill to learn.

On the other hand, **wants** are the nice-to-haves, the extras, the cherries on top. Wants include expenses like eating out, buying a new video game, or going to the movies with your friends. Wants also include your big goals, like taking a trip to Europe or saving for your own car.

The trick to effective budgeting is striking a balance between your needs and wants. It's about covering your needs first and then seeing how much you have left for your wants.

Fixed and Variable Expenses

Okay, not to be confused with 'needs' and 'wants', which are two ways to categorize your expenses, we're going to talk about the two main types of expenses you'll encounter in budgeting - fixed and variable expenses. These are subcategories, where all of your needs and wants will fit into either fixed or variable expenses. Picture them as two sides of a coin, each distinct yet part of the same whole. They're both expenses, they just get budgeted differently.

Fixed expenses are the costs that stay the same each month, such as rent payments, car payments, phone payments, or insurance premiums.

Variable expenses, as the name suggests, change from month to month. These include things like groceries, gas, utilities, and personal care expenses.

When planning your budget, you need to account for both fixed and variable expenses. However, fixed expenses will be a lot easier to plan for. This will give you a complete picture of where your money is going and help you make informed decisions about your spending.

When it comes to variable expenses, think of the *most* you might spend that month and plan for that. That way, you may have extra money at the end of the month instead of not having enough to cover everything if you plan for a lower amount.

This might be hard to visualize, so I'll give an example. Let's say you spent $36 on snacks in January. You spent $48 on snacks in February and $32 in March. When planning (aka budgeting) this variable expense for future months, enter $50 into your budget. That will ensure you have enough to cover the expense based on your past spending, but you may have some extra money at the end of the month (bonus). Make sense?

Track Your Spending

To budget properly, you need to know where every cent of your money is. Start today by keeping a record of every purchase, no matter how small. You could use a simple notebook, a spreadsheet, or even a budgeting app (there's a page in the workbook, too!). Make a note of what you bought, how much it cost, and which category it falls into (needs or wants, fixed or variable). Do this for one month to start. This record is a snapshot of your spending habits. It shows where your money is going, which areas are draining your wallet, and where you might need to cut back.

Unless you're using the workbook (page 91), write out the following categories and use your tracking sheet to tally your spending in each category.

- Groceries

- Eating out and snacks

- Transportation (Car payment, gas, insurance, bus tickets, etc.)

- Cell phone

- Subscriptions (Netflix, Spotify, etc.)

- Entertainment (movies, concerts, video games, etc.)

- Shopping (clothes, accessories, etc)

- Hobbies and activities

- Education (books, fees, etc.)

- Health and personal care

- Savings

When you're done, look over these categories and determine if the amount you're spending seems appropriate or if it's something you can cut back on.

Keep this tracking sheet handy. Coming up, we're going to use it to plan out a workable budget. In the meantime, keep tracking your spending. Tracking your spending is a skill you will want to continue... forever.

Saving for the Rainy Day: True Financial Responsibility

Okay, so we've talked about expenses, or spending money. That's the easy part! Now, let's dig into saving money. Oof - I know that can be hard.

Importance of Saving

Why is it a good idea to stash away part of your allowance or paycheck instead of spending it all? Here's the deal. Let's say you want to buy a car. The car you want is $4,000 (it may be beaten up and old, but since it has wheels, it's the car of your dreams, right?). Unless somehow you win the lottery or are gifted $4,000 all at once, you'll have to save up some money over time if you ever hope to buy that car.

Saving up for something you want isn't the only reason to put money aside. Sometimes in life, unexpected expenses come up - like you might need new tires on that sweet ride a year after you buy it, or tuition is due, but you're in between jobs. If you don't have money saved, you'll either have to rely on credit (which we'll talk about later), or you'll have to go without. Neither of these are great options. Having money set aside for a "rainy day" is smart and can feel like a lifesaver in certain situations.

Having savings gives you financial freedom. It's like having a safety net under your tightrope. You can walk more confidently, knowing that if you stumble, you'll be caught. It allows you to make choices, take calculated risks, and grab opportunities without fearing financial fallout.

Setting Financial Goals

Alright, now that you know why saving is crucial, let's talk about how to do it effectively. And it all starts with setting financial goals. Think of it as your destination on a road trip. Without knowing exactly where you're headed, you'll never end up where you want to be.

Your financial goals could be as short-term as buying that new video game, as medium-term as saving up for that fire car, or as long-term as putting money away for college. The point is to have a clear target, something tangible that you're saving for.

Once you've set your goal, break it down into manageable chunks. If your goal is to save $600 for a new guitar in a year, that breaks down to saving $50 monthly or about $12 weekly. Suddenly, that big, scary goal seems much more achievable, right?

Take a minute right now and write down some financial goals (there's space in the workbook - page 93). Make sure you have a good idea of how much those goals will cost (the total amount you need to save), then break it down. If you get paid twice a month, I suggest breaking down your savings by paycheck. So, instead of the $12 a week for the guitar, you'd be looking at more like $24 per paycheck. Make sense?

Now, what if one of your financial goals is more long-term and expensive, like eventually buying a house or saving for retirement (hey - if your goal is to start saving for retirement now, you are amazing! I highly recommend it!). You may not have a solid number or a set amount of time, so you can't calculate exactly how much you should save. Instead, decide on a set dollar amount or percentage that you will set aside with each paycheck and stick with it. I recommend making it a percentage so that no matter how much your income is, you can always put this amount aside. A good percentage to save is about 10% of every paycheck for longer-term savings.

Compound Interest

There's a magical phenomenon in the world of finance - it's called compound interest. It's like a snowball making its way down a hill. It starts small, but as it rolls down, it picks up more snow, growing bigger and faster.

Here's how it works. The bank pays you interest when you save money in a savings account. Interest is just the bank's way of saying, "Hey, if you let us keep your money for you, we'll put a little bit into your account each month as a thank you."

If you were to put $100 into a savings account, and the bank says they'll pay you 4% interest, then at the end of the first month, you'd have $100.33. That .33 cents doesn't feel like much, but - it's free money! If you leave that $100.33 in your account, the next time they calculate interest, they do it on the original amount plus the interest you've already earned. So, you earn interest on your interest. That's compound interest.

Using the $100 example, you'd have $104.35 in that savings account at the end of one year. It's not much when you only have $100 in your account, but it is money you didn't have to earn, and that's with putting nothing else into the account all year. Ideally, you'll keep adding to your savings every month, which means the interest you'll earn will also increase. The more you save, the more you earn in interest.

The magic of compound interest is in its ability to grow your money exponentially over time. It's like planting a small seed and watching it grow into a massive tree. But for the magic to work, you need two things - regular savings and time. The more regularly you save and the longer you let your money grow, the more powerful the magic of compound interest.

Create a Workable Budget

So here's where the rubber meets the road. You're going to put everything you just learned together to create a real-life budget that will work for you.

Pull out your expense tracking sheet so you have a reference for what you need to budget for the future, and either your workbook (page 95), piece of paper, or note on your phone. You can also use a good app if you prefer a digital form. Follow the steps below to create your budget.

1. Determine your income and write it at the top. If you get paychecks multiple times a month, write down how much you get with each paycheck. If you make a different amount every month, determine the *lowest* amount you might make in a month and budget using this number (anything extra is gravy).

2. Using your tracking sheet from above, list each category applicable to you on separate lines.

3. Using your actual spending habits as a guide (from your tracking sheet),

start filling out the categories with an amount that is aligned with your goals (like maybe you were spending $80 a month on fast food but have decided spending $50 a month is more reasonable.)

    a. Start with your **fixed needs** first, as these are categories for which you know the exact amount you have to pay, and it will remain the same every month.

    b. Then, move on to your **variable needs**. Use the *most* you think you would pay monthly (like that $50 for snacks example).

    c. Add in your **savings** goal. If you don't have anything you're saving for, calculate 10% of your income and write this number down.

    d. Now, start filling in your **wants**. Start with what feels most important to you. If you love to get a soda with your friends once a week, calculate how much you think is appropriate to spend in a month and write that down.

    e. Continue filling in your wants until you've reached your income level. You can't budget for spending $500 when you're only making $475 each month.

You have two options if you have more needs or wants than you have money for. 1: get a better paying job, or 2: spend less. If you want to be financially savvy, those are your options.

Now that you have a budget worked out that is exactly matched for you, be sure to follow it! Look at it often, and always before you go out to spend money. Discipline yourself to stick to your budget and watch the world open up to you. If your budget isn't working for you after a month or two, feel free to reassess and make changes. This is how you'll learn to master your money and be the envy of all your friends when you can do things down the road that they could never imagine.

Building Financial Credit

At some point, you'll want to start building financial credit. There are different types of credit: credit cards, loans for things like cars and houses, and student loans are all examples of using credit. But you can only buy a car using credit if you have already established yourself as a responsible money handler. Using credit can get you into a whole world of trouble if you're not smart, so it's not something I recommend doing early on, but it is something you'll want to think about.

My husband and I bought our first home months before I turned 20 (yes - we were married very young!). We could only do this because I had established good credit as a teenager. Establishing credit at a young age is a great financial strategy only IF you are mature enough to handle it. *If you struggle to manage and budget your money, hold off on getting a credit card* or using credit until you are able to have a good handle on how to budget and spend responsibly.

Understanding Credit Score

Think of your favorite video game. You start at level one, and as you navigate through challenges, defeat enemies, and collect rewards, you level up. Now, imagine a similar game, but this one plays out in the financial world. It's called establishing a financial credit score, and it's not exactly a game, but we're going to go with that.

Your credit score is a three-digit number that tells banks and lenders how reliable you are when it comes to handling money. It's like your report card in the credit score game, and the aim is to score as high as possible. For reference, an 800 credit score is pretty hype. Make that your goal.

A good credit score can open up a world of opportunities. It can help you get approved for credit cards, qualify for loans with lower interest rates, and even make it easier to rent an apartment.

Credit scores are calculated using several factors, including your payment history (do you pay the full amount on time?), the amount of debt you owe (less debt = higher score), the length of your credit history (how long have you had good credit), and more. It's a complex algorithm in the credit score game, and understanding how it works can give you an edge.

You can start building a credit score by getting a simple credit card (that's what I did when I was 17), or if you're in college, check with your apartment complex to see if they have a program that will help you build credit by reporting your monthly rent payments. This is a great way to build credit without any risk.

Responsible Credit Card Use

One of the ways to build your credit score is through responsible credit card use. If done wisely, credit card use can boost your score and open up opportunities. Used recklessly, it can knock you back and make you miserable. Like, truly miserable, so please be careful.

First of all, how does a credit card work? A bank or credit card company will check your financial history, and if you're approved, they'll issue you a card with a specific limit to the amount you can spend - maybe something like $500. This means you can spend up to $500 using the card. You have to pay off the money you spend, but you can do it over time. If you pay it all off within the first month, you won't be charged anything extra (called interest). But conversely, for any amount you do not pay off within the month, you'll have to pay interest to the bank.

Interest is the fee the bank charges for using their money, and these interest rates are very high; you'll want to avoid paying them at all costs.

Here's the key to using a credit card responsibly: treat it like a debit card. Only spend what you can afford to pay off in full each month. This shows lenders that you can manage debt responsibly, which can help improve your credit score and keep you out of financial ruin.

Also, aim to keep your credit utilization low. This is the percentage of your available credit that you're using. For example, suppose your credit card has a limit of $1,000, and you have a balance of $500. In that case, your credit utilization is 50%. As a rule of thumb, try to keep this ratio below 30%.

Do not use a credit card to buy whatever you've been longing for, thinking you can pay for it over time. Use what you learned above about saving for those wants, and only use your credit card to help you build credit. I highly recommend you always pay off your credit card in full every month. This will help you maintain a high credit score and prevent you from paying interest to the credit card company, which is just throwing your money away.

If you're still confused and wondering what the point is of having a credit card just to pay it off every month, it's so you can establish a credit history and credit score for things like buying a house, paying rent, or buying a car. That's it. Having good credit is necessary, but you have to be smart about it. I cannot overemphasize this enough: if you struggle with handling money, please do not get a credit card. Work on following a budget, and when you feel you are a budgeting pro, then consider starting to build credit.

Real-Life Money Scenarios and How to Handle Them

Dealing with Financial Emergencies

Sometimes, life throws you a curveball in the form of financial emergencies. They're like pop quizzes in the school of life - unexpected, stressful, and demanding quick thinking. Hopefully, as a teen, you won't have many financial emergencies. Still, they could come in the form of a broken phone or laptop, a stolen bike, or suddenly having to get new tires on your car.

In a financial emergency, the first step is to stay calm. Take a deep breath, channel your inner Zen master, and assess the situation. Ask yourself, "What are my options? What resources do I have at my disposal? Who can I turn to for help?"

Next, explore possible solutions. Can you borrow a friend's laptop or use one at a public library? Can you use public transport or carpool with a friend until you can afford a new bike? Remember, the goal is not to solve the problem overnight but to manage it effectively without breaking your budget or losing your mind.

Remember when we talked about "saving for a rainy day"? Consider setting up an emergency fund: a stash of money set aside specifically for unexpected expenses. Even a small amount saved regularly can add up over time and really come in handy when you need it most.

Managing Peer Pressure Spending

Here's a very real but tricky scenario: peer pressure spending. It's the tug-of-war between your budget and your desire to fit in. Imagine your friends are raving about the latest designer sneakers or planning a pricey weekend getaway. You want to join in, but your wallet screams, "No way!"

Start by being honest with yourself and your friends about your financial situation. You don't have to spill all the beans; just a simple "I can't afford it right now" or "I'm saving up for something else" should do the trick. True friends will understand and respect your decision.

Next, suggest affordable alternatives. Instead of dining at a fancy restaurant for the school dance, why not host a nice dinner at home? Rather than splurge on concert tickets, why not organize a movie night? It's about finding creative ways to have fun without busting your budget. But if you are dying to go to that concert, start saving early so it's not an issue.

Finally, remember that it's okay to say no. Resisting peer pressure can be tough, but taking control of your financial life is worth it. Stay true to your budget and financial goals, and let your 'no' be a stepping stone towards financial independence.

Chapter 11

Shop Right - Cook Right - Eat Right

In Chapter 7, you learned about the importance of nutrition and how to read food labels. Now, we will put that nutrition knowledge into a workable skill so that when the time comes, you can adult like you know how, and eat like royalty.

Food fuels our bodies, sharpens our minds, and gives us the energy to conquer our daily battles. You might have mom or dad buying and preparing your food for now, but being able to shop and cook for yourself is a necessary skill - unless you plan to live off of fast food your entire life, which isn't a good idea for multiple reasons (not only will that blow your budget, but it'll probably blow your belt buckle as well. No bueno).

I will walk you through the steps you need to succeed so that when you're off on your own, you know exactly how to feed yourself nutritious meals. I encourage you, however, to practice these skills *now*. Help your parents make a meal plan, go with them to the grocery store, start by helping to make meals, and then occasionally practice making meals all on your own.

While you're still living at home, gather your favorite family recipes: write them down and practice making them. When you're living on your own, making recipes from your youth will bring comfort and a warm feeling. You won't regret taking the time now to practice making your favorite meals!

I've created a companion book called "Mom's Go-To Recipes and Journal," where I've shared several of my family's favorite quick and easy recipes and have given you space to write in your family's favorite recipes as well. The ones I've shared are quick, easy, and inexpensive to make and are the same recipes my college boy makes on the regular. If you need some quick and easy ideas, that's a good place to start. You can also do an internet search for quick and simple recipes, though the results might be overwhelming.

Meal Planning

Planning out the food you will eat throughout your week may be the most important step of them all when it comes to living and eating on your own. Without a plan, you'll be roaming the grocery store like a hunter and gatherer, likely to buy mostly highly processed foods that look good at the moment, only to return home and not have a clue what you're going to actually eat and you'll end up going for take-out anyway. Not a wise way to spend your money or your time. Planning leads to success.

If you're not already a foodie who loves to cook, making a meal plan can feel daunting. The best way to overcome this feeling is to keep it super simple. You don't need to be eating like a king every day, and if you don't mind leftovers, you can cook once and eat all week. A word to those that don't like leftovers - I see you. I would encourage you to try out different foods as leftovers, as some may be great the next day or two, while others just become unappetizing. I get it. Play around with it because leftovers can save you a whole lot of time and brain power.

Make Your Meal Plan

The first step to making a meal plan is to know your budget. So go back to the budget you've created and see how much you have allotted for groceries. If you're not buying your own food just yet, do this exercise with your parents using their food budget, or you can do this exercise for yourself using a mock budget.

Food prices continue to go up, which is concerning, but I can tell you that in early 2024, my college student spends about $50 a week on groceries. He's very health conscious and makes most of his own food, though he does eat out for a few meals each week, which is an added expense. If you have no idea how much to budget for food, that might give you a good idea for a starting point. However, assuming you're not living on your own yet, go ahead and talk to your mom or dad about the monthly food budget and help them devise a plan.

You can plan out one week at a time or even a month. If you don't mind repeating meals, you can plan out one week and simply repeat that same week the entire month. Save each of your meal plans so you can reuse them down the road. You'll likely want to change things up as seasons change, but otherwise, eating many of the same meals over and over for a couple months is a great way to meal plan the easy way.

There's space in the workbook (page 99) to help you plan out a week of meals; otherwise, get out your paper or make a note on your phone. Start by making a list of meals that you enjoy. Just write them down as you think of them. For those still at home, making a list of meals you enjoy is a great first step to preparing for when you move out on your own. Continue adding to this list whenever you think of a meal you like. If you have the companion recipe book, this is the perfect place to write down those recipes.

Next, using your list of favorite meals, start filling in a weekly meal plan. Breakfast, lunch, dinner, and you can add snacks and dessert if you'd like. Remember, repeating is a-okay and even encouraged! Think about what you can make for dinner one night and possibly eat for lunch or dinner the next day. In our house, we always eat leftovers from dinner for lunch the following day. Always. Cook once, eat (at least) twice! It will save you money and time!

Create a Grocery List

Now that you have your meal plan, you need to create a grocery list, so you know exactly what you need to buy at the store. You can make a note on your phone using a checklist format, which is a great thing to take to the grocery store to mark them off as you put items in your cart.

Go through each meal, one by one, and write down all the groceries you need. Bonus: If you've created a meal plan that reuses many of the same ingredients, that will save you some money! Don't forget snacks like fresh fruit, yogurt, cheese sticks - whatever isn't a part of your meals that you can grab when you just need a quick bite. Be specific on your list - so instead of writing "fresh fruit," write "5 bananas" or "3 apples". With a list like that, you're ready to slay the grocery store like a ninja.

For those still at home and eating whatever mom or dad prepares, don't think you're exempt from learning these skills until you move out! Help your parents make a meal plan and grocery shop now so that you're already a pro when you move out, and it won't feel scary!

Grocery Shopping

Once you have your meal plan and grocery list, it's time to tackle the grocery store. A successful grocery trip is one in which you come away with everything on your list while staying at or under budget. That might take some practice. If you've gone way over budget your first week, you may need to look at your upcoming meal plan and see if there are other meals you could make that might use fewer ingredients, or snacks that you could cut out. Or you may need to readjust your budget to better align with your food requirements.

As you're shopping, I recommend adding up the cost as you put items in your cart so you know exactly how much you're spending and when you've reached your budget. Get the ingredients on your grocery list first, and then, if you have leftover money, you can add snacks and treats to your cart.

While shopping, there are a few tricks to be mindful of that will help you get the most out of your money and make you look like you know exactly what you're doing there.

The first trick is to never go to the grocery store hungry. That's a recipe for disaster as everything (especially the sugary, salty snacks) will be calling out to you, and you'll end up spending way more than you planned and getting food that doesn't align with your goals.

Understanding Store Layout

Trick two is cracking the code of the grocery store layout. Once you understand it, navigating the aisles becomes a breeze. Most grocery stores follow a similar layout. Essential items like fruits, vegetables, dairy, and meat are usually located around the store's perimeter. Why? Because these items are replaced frequently, and having them on the outer edges allows easy access for restocking.

In contrast, packaged foods, snacks, and beverages often occupy the inner aisles. And strategically placed at eye level are the most popular - and often pricier - brands. Have you ever noticed how sugary cereals are at kids' eye level while healthier options are placed higher up? That's no accident! Understanding these tactics can help you make smarter choices and avoid falling into marketing traps.

Start by shopping the perimeter for the fresh items you need, then wind your way through the inner isles to get the canned and packaged foods on your list. The more you shop, the more familiar you'll get with your store's layout and the easier it will be to find exactly what you need.

Stick to your list. If you find that going to the grocery store sets you up for overbuying food that's not on your list, try using online shopping to avoid those impulse buys completely.

Seasonal Shopping

Trick three is buying fruits and vegetables that are in season. When a particular fruit or vegetable is in season, there's an abundance of it, which leads to lower prices. Plus, seasonal produce is typically fresher and tastier. It's grown under optimal conditions, allowed to ripen naturally, and doesn't have to travel long distances to reach the store. So, next time you're in the produce aisle, think seasonal, not just colorful.

Buying in Bulk

The next trick is to buy in bulk. Buying in bulk can save you money on items you use frequently with a long shelf life. Think of staples like rice, pasta, canned goods, or even toilet paper. These items are often cheaper when bought in larger quantities. If you see something you frequently use is on sale, that's a great time to purchase that item in bulk. But, don't go overboard. Remember, the goal is to stock up, not to hoard. And be wary of perishable items. Buying fresh produce or dairy products in bulk might lead to waste if you can't consume them in time.

Store Brand vs Name Brand

Finally, let's tackle the age-old debate - store brand or name brand? Store brands, also known as private labels, are often just as good as their name-brand counterparts. In many cases, they're even manufactured in the same facilities as the name brands! The main difference? Marketing. Name brands spend a lot on advertising and pass these costs on to the consumer. Sometimes, there may be a slight difference in ingredients or flavor between the store brand or name brand, but I would encourage you to try the store brand, as you may even prefer the taste of it!

You'll want to put all your groceries away as soon as you get home, especially the foods that need to go in the fridge or freezer. It's good practice to store items separately from each other in the fridge - like keeping your raw meats away from your produce. If you're not going to be using your raw meats in the next few days, storing them in the freezer and thawing them the day you need them will ensure they don't go bad before you get to cooking them.

Meal Prep Like a Pro

So you have your meal plan, you've done your grocery shopping, and now all that's left is to follow your plan and cook your meals. Cooking is a skill learned by practicing (just like every other skill), and sometimes, you'll have small or even significant failures. Failing is part of the learning process, so don't be too hard on yourself. Just make the best of a failed situation and try again later. You'll be surprised how much you'll learn from those frustrating failures, so don't give up when they happen.

Kitchen Basics and Safety

I prefer to always start off by having a clean kitchen, and I suggest you do that as well. You don't want to have to wash a pan right when you need it or be searching for the spatula at the bottom of a dirty sink. Wash all the dirty dishes and wipe down your counters before you start cooking. You'll be glad you did. And while you're at it, ensure your hands are washed as well. Cause... Ick.

When I'm making a meal, I like to get all the ingredients out and have them on the counter, so I don't have to go searching for something while I'm in the middle of the recipe. So get out all your ingredients, cooking utensils, and pots or pans that you'll need and have everything ready.

You'll want to wash all your produce before cutting them. I like to cut the produce all at once before I get started with any actual cooking so they're all ready to go. You can put them in individual bowls or keep them in piles on the cutting board until you're ready to add them to your cooking. Another tip is to cut your produce as soon as you get home from the grocery store and keep everything in a container in the fridge until you're ready to use it. If you have some extra time after getting home from the grocery store, try it out and see how awesome you feel later in the week when you have pre-cut produce ready for your recipe.

As a general kitchen safety rule, you should always have quick access to a fire extinguisher in the kitchen, and know how to use it. Grease catches fire quickly and is not put out by water, so keep your stovetop and oven clean and free from grease.

You'll learn the following skills best by having someone teach you hands-on. So grab a parent, grandparent, or friend who knows how (and with parental permission), and have them teach you the following skills. At the very least though, you can watch a YouTube video to show you each skill. You can take your time with this and learn a new skill once or twice a week, or just go all in and learn them all at once. If something feels tricky or is frustrating, just remember, the only way you'll ever get better is to practice, so don't give up!

- Proper knife handling and storage
- How to cut a variety of vegetables
- How to boil a pot of water
- How to use appliances like the oven or stovetop
- The difference between boiling, pan frying, baking, grilling, and sauteing
- How to identify kitchen tools like a spatula, pot, pan, and measuring cups
- How to use a kitchen timer

There's a page in the workbook (page 105) to mark off each of these skills as you learn them. You can also take notes about what you learned. The biggest thing to do now is to practice! So go get cooking!

Batch Cooking

Batch cooking is preparing multiple servings of a meal at once and storing them for later use. So, instead of cooking every day, you cook once or twice a week, and voila! You have ready-made meals whenever you need them. Try making one or two extra servings each time you cook and store the leftovers in the fridge or the freezer if it'll be a while before you are ready to eat it.

This works really well for things like soups, pasta, rice, and sauces. Once cooked, portion them into meal-sized containers, ready to be reheated when hunger strikes. It's like having your own line of ready meals, minus the preservatives and the hefty price tag.

Safe Food Storage

Whether you batch cook or just store leftovers for later, you need to be mindful of proper food storage. When storing cooked food, always wait for it to cool to room temperature. Hot food can raise the temperature of your fridge, putting everything else at risk of spoiling.

Next, store your food in airtight containers, which will protect your food from air and moisture. This keeps your food fresh and prevents flavors and smells from mingling. After all, nobody wants their blueberry muffins to taste like garlic prawns! Bonus points if you use glass over plastic containers, as some plastics can leach into your food over time. Gross.

Lastly, keep an eye on storage times. Even in the fridge, cooked food doesn't last forever. As a rule of thumb, consume refrigerated cooked food within 3 to 4 days. For more extended storage, consider freezing. Remember to label and date your containers to know what's what and when it was stored.

Chapter 12

Keep It Clean, Please

I n my house, I've got one kiddo who loves a clean, organized space and another who seems to love chaos. Interestingly, the one that likes to clean also has fewer mental struggles as well. That may or may not be a case of cause and effect, but studies have shown that a clean environment can undoubtedly contribute to mental well-being. Knowing how to clean, and living in an orderly environment has several long-term benefits. For one, it shows responsibility and respect, not only for yourself but for others. It promotes better health and is an indication of good hygiene. Keeping your areas clean frees up time and space for other activities. And while you may not think it does, knowing how to clean and being organized can affect your ability to get and maintain a job. I'm not saying you have to become a neat-freak, but knowing how to maintain a clean environment is an important life skill worth practicing.

Declutter Your Space To Simplify Your Life

The spaces we inhabit often become a reflection of the chaos of our minds. When we accumulate possessions - stuff - things - we can feel weighed down both physically and mentally. Decluttering is a process that is more than just putting things away so our space feels and looks clean; it's a practice of shedding the unnecessary and making our lives simpler in the process.

So, the first step to mastering the life skill of cleanliness is to start by decluttering your space. This means going through your stuff and deciding what to keep, what to donate, and what to throw away. You might be surprised at how much stuff you have that you don't actually need or use. Get rid of clothes that don't fit, old school papers you no longer need, and books you read as a 6-year-old. For those somewhat sentimental items - like that purple and gold, slightly off-center clay bowl you made in 3rd grade that you'll never use - take a picture of it for memory sake and then toss it out. The alternative is to keep it in a box for the next 35 years and move it around with you. Do you really want to carry it from house to house for the next 35 years? Of course, the choice is truly yours, but think about it.

If this feels very overwhelming, just choose one spot or location to declutter first. Maybe it's that one corner of your closet where things go to die, or one or two drawers. Or maybe just your bookcase, and don't forget about underneath your bed. Make a list of "locations" and work through them one at a time.

Decluttering is something that you'll do over and over throughout your life. We live in a society where we accumulate stuff very easily and quickly. Most things we hold on to have some meaning initially, but as we grow and change, it's okay to let go of things that were once important to us but now serve no purpose in our lives and just take up space. Make a goal to go through the decluttering process once or twice a year. Your parents, friends that come to hang out, future roommates, employers, and spouse will thank you!

Go ahead and get that workbook (page 107)/phone note/piece of paper out and make a list of locations you want to declutter. You could have just a few bigger locations or make a long list of small locations. Once you have your list, determine a timeline for how long you'd like to take to get it all done, or determine one day a week that you'll dedicate 15-30 minutes to one location. Work through your locations one by one until you've successfully decluttered. If you feel like it's too much and you find yourself giving up, take it down a notch instead of giving up altogether. Set a shorter time limit or determine a smaller location. Don't give up on the process because it feels hard - instead, make it doable for you.

Organizing: Where Everything Has a Place

Ever heard the phrase, "A place for everything, and everything in its place"? Well, it's about to become your organizing mantra. If you always know where your stuff is, you'll save precious time and energy looking for and cleaning up things, and you'll stop making yourself and others crazy in the process.

Start by identifying 'homes' for your items. The home for your books could be a shelf, your clothes could live in your closet, your school supplies could have a drawer, and your dirty laundry lives in the laundry basket. Choose a home for each item or collection of items and set that home in stone. The key here is consistency. Always return items to their homes after using them. If you get something new, find it a home immediately. Use bins, boxes, or shelves to group similar items together. Label each container so you can easily find what you're looking for. Make sure to store frequently used items in easily accessible places.

Now that everything has a home, make sure it's organized neatly within its home. A bookshelf where all the book spines can be seen is so much more delightful than a bookshelf where all the books are stacked randomly. A drawer of folded shirts feels much nicer than a drawer of crumpled balls of shirt-like items. However, if all you can do now is get those shirts in the right drawer, call that a win and tackle bigger organization skills as you're ready. Progress is progress! Don't get discouraged.

If you always put things away in their home before dropping them on the floor or tossing them on your desk, you'll save yourself time and mental and physical energy in the long run. It's a simple habit that can keep your space organized and clutter-free. Remember, the goal of organizing isn't to make your space look like a magazine spread. It's to make your life easier. So, create an organizational system that works for you, not against you.

Take some time now to look around your space and create homes for each of your items. Even if you've already decluttered, if you come across something as you're organizing that you feel you don't really need, I encourage you to get rid of it. Keep your spaces in mind when acquiring new items. If you don't have room for something new, consider if it's something you really need.

Laundry 101

My kids started doing their own laundry around the age of nine. Shockingly, during high school and even into college, my oldest told me several times how grateful he was that I had taught him to do his own laundry because many of his friends didn't know how. If you're not already doing your laundry, this is one skill you can quickly master, and it will have you feeling like a true adulting expert in no time. Granted, I know how nice it is to have someone do your laundry for you, but if you don't practice now, you'll be the one in college feeling like a dork because all your clothes have a pink tint to them because of some sort of laundry mishap.

There are varying degrees of laundry care. Some people like to hand wash some clothes or line dry others. This is dependent on how precious you feel your clothes are. If you buy a lot of silk, satin, or delicate items, you'll probably want to take special care when washing those clothes. Or if you're worried about clothes shrinking, which can happen significantly with natural fibers such as cotton, wool, silk, and linen. In that case, you might want to line dry those items (that means you don't put them in the dryer but instead hang them to dry). Clothes tags will indicate if an item should be washed or dried in a particular manner, so it's a good idea to check the tag on your clothes before washing them for the first time. Or you may be like me and my family, and you simply don't own precious clothing. For those of you, everything will go in the washer, and everything will go in the dryer, but there are still some things to be aware of, which we'll get to in a bit.

Before we get into the nitty-gritty of how to do your laundry, I just want to mention - because I'm a mom, and I know - that you don't need to wash every piece of clothing or every towel after a single use. In fact, did you know that denim jeans are meant to be worn repeatedly without washing? It's true - they were created for that purpose. And using a towel once after a shower does not make it dirty. Hang it up to dry and use it for a week. It's not gross. But since you're so keen on washing *everything*, don't forget about your bed sheets. Those should be washed weekly. If you deal with acne, it's wise to wash your pillowcase daily (or turn your pillow over each night so you can wash the case every other day).

Okay, so let's get into it. Most people will tell you that you must sort your laundry into lights, darks, and whites before washing, but I will tell you a secret. Wash whites separately, yes, but the rest can all be thrown in together, given a few rules:

1. Wash dark jeans separately. The color will bleed onto any other piece of clothing in the load, and you'll have a wardrobe of blue clothes.

2. Wash new red items separately several times before eventually adding them to your colored load. Same idea as the bleeding jeans - but everything will be pink.

3. Don't overload the washer. If you have too many clothes to fit com-

fortably in the washer without shoving more in, create separate piles of medium-sized loads.

4. Washing towels separately isn't a must, but I'd recommend washing towels and sheets in the same load by themselves. Both washed once a week, so it works, wink.

5. When washing whites, make sure you don't have a stray colored sock in with the load. Make sure it's all whites, or you may end up with pink or blue "whites."

Treating Stains

If you have grass, blood, grease, or... poo on your clothes, you'll want to pretreat those before throwing them in the washer. You can use special sprays meant to pretreat laundry stains or hand soap if you don't have any sprays on hand. Let the soap sit on the stain for several minutes, then scrub the soap into the stain. If you use a laundry stain remover, you can then throw that directly into the washer. If you use hand soap, rinse it out thoroughly before throwing it in the washer.

Using Bleach

Only use bleach on white clothes unless you want your colored clothes to turn white. Bleach will actually turn your white clothes slightly yellow, and I personally recommend *never* using bleach in your laundry. If you have a stain, treat the stain directly with a stain remover product. Bleach isn't necessary in laundry, and it just dumps bleach into the water system, so I'd recommend just staying away from it.

Okay, so now you've got your pile of laundry with stains treated, and you're ready to wash them. Add your detergent to the washer, then add your clothes. There are so many detergent options that you'll have to read on the package how much to add. Of course, whether it's a powdered or liquid detergent, you'll add more for bigger cycles and less for smaller ones. No need to go crazy with the detergent - just add the appropriate amount.

The options on a washer include the water temperature and the type of cycle. As a general rule, use hot water for whites, warm water for colors, and cold water for those jeans, reds, and any delicate fabrics. Hot water will allow for more shrinkage and color bleed, but will also get your clothes slightly cleaner. So, think about what your goal is for each load. The type of cycle will also vary depending on what kind of washing machine you're dealing with, but the "regular" or sometimes called "normal" cycle is usually sufficient unless it's delicates you're washing, then of course, the delicate cycle will work best. The heavy cycle is great if you have stains or very dirty clothes.

Now, on to the dryer. Again, hot air will shrink clothes better than cooler air, so keep that in mind. If you're drying delicates or fabrics more prone to shrinkage, a cooler temperature setting is more appropriate. If you're in my family, it's high heat for long time. Boom. Laundry done.

Let's talk about all those fun things you can add to the washer and dryer. You've got products that make your clothes smell yummy and products that soften clothes or keep them from getting sticky. Fabric softener actually breaks down the fibers of your clothes, so I don't recommend it if you want your clothes to stay looking decent. And I know how nice it is to have yummy-smelling clothes, but I want you to think about the ingredients in these kinds of products. They're all chemicals. These chemicals get in your clothes and will get on your skin, and can potentially cause all sorts of health issues after time. They also cost extra money you really don't need to spend to have clean clothes. Obviously, the decision is up to you, but be aware they're unnecessary. If you live in a dry climate, static cling can be a real issue, especially in winter. Instead of using chemical-laden and expensive dryer sheets, you can purchase reusable fabric sheets or balls that can go in your dryer to help keep your clothes from getting that static cling. This is a great way to save money and keep dryer sheets out of landfills.

Once your clothes are clean and dry, you're not done yet! Don't forget about folding and putting away! Folding your clothes makes them wrinkle-free and easier to store in your drawers. There are YouTube videos on how to fold clothes, and you'll find many different methods. All methods are great. Far superior to shoving clothes in your drawers or letting them sit in the laundry basket until they're used again.

Ironing Clothes

I know wrinkled clothes might not seem like a big deal, and honestly, in many situations, you can get away with a lot of wrinkles and not have to worry about it. But every once in a while, you're going to have a severely wrinkled shirt that has no hope unless it's properly ironed. You can minimize wrinkles if you take your clothes out of the dryer while still warm and fold or hang them immediately, so there's value to staying on top of your laundry game. But sometimes you need to look your best, and your best shirt looks like a crumpled ball.

Learning to use an iron safely and correctly is a life skill you might not think you need, but you'll be glad to know. And if ironing clothes sounds like something you'll never do, you can iron other things, like Perler beads, so knowing how to use an iron is still useful, wink. My kids have loved creating with Perler beads and learned to use an iron at a young age so they could create all they wanted (although we did have one ironing disaster that involved melting the carpet... don't do that). Craft projects aside, learning to use an iron is a life skill I think you'll want to know.

So first things first, when using an iron, never put it hot side down on *anything*! Especially carpet. Or your hands. Always keep it standing up on a safe surface (like the ironing board), and keep your hands away from the hot metal. While ironing, you'll keep the iron moving, instead of setting it on the fabric for any amount of time. This will prevent any potential burns to the item you're ironing. The next important skill is to always unplug an iron after you're done using it, even if it has a self-shut-off timer. If you remember those important rules when using an iron, you're most of the way there.

Now, there's a particular way to iron a men's dress shirt properly, and I'm not going to lie - the collar is still hard for me to get right, so don't feel bad if it takes you awhile to figure it out. Watch a YouTube video or two and practice, practice, practice. Women's blouses are much easier, though be sure to use the appropriate iron temperature based on the type of fabric. Pants are much easier, so practicing on pants might be a good idea before moving on to shirts.

Looking your best, with ironed clothes, will help you to feel your best, especially on special occasions. Don't put off learning how to use an iron. This is a skill that you can definitely master as a teen.

Clean It Like You Mean It

We're talking about clean surroundings now. I know that for teenagers (and for some reason, especially boys), it's easy to look past the gross-ness you're living in and think it's someone else's problem to clean. But if you can get into a habit of cleaning now, you'll be the one the girls want to visit (and not be afraid to use the toilet), and you'll be the roommate others will want to have. Keeping a clean environment shows good hygiene, good manners, and respect for others and yourself. If you keep up with regular cleaning, it never becomes so gross and daunting that you would rather burn the place down than clean it up.

So, let's list some of the basics of what to clean. These are in no particular order:

1. Make your bed. It takes 20 seconds and can make you feel completely different. Try it out and notice how you feel with a clean, made-up bed.

2. Dust. It will help keep allergies down, and it sure looks gross when a surface hasn't been dusted in a while.

3. Vacuum and sweep. This might be my top tip: Everything looks cleaner

when the floors are clean. If you're having people over, make vacuuming and sweeping a top priority. Likewise, clean up spills immediately, as stained flooring makes everything look dirty and gross.

4. Mop. Once a month or so, make sure you deep clean those floors by mopping.

5. Bathroom maintenance. For the love, please scrub your toilet inside and out (and if you're a boy, the walls and floors surrounding it). Scrub that bathtub. Wipe down the mirror, sink, faucet, and counter. The more often you do this, the easier it will be. Don't let it get super gross. At the very least, you can use bleach wipes to wipe everything down each night and then do a serious deep clean once a month.

6. Kitchen maintenance. If you go to bed with a clean kitchen, you'll wake up to a clean kitchen every single day! Wink. Wipe down the counters, sink, faucet, and load all dishes in the dishwasher daily. Run the dishwasher as needed at night and empty it first thing the following day so you can reload it as needed. Wipe down the kitchen table after each use.

7. Take out the trash. You've waited too long if it's starting to spill over or smell. Take out the garbage once a week on the same day, and you won't have to think about it otherwise.

Obviously, some of these are more geared to those who have moved out of mom and dad's house. But even if you're still at home, look at the list and see what you can do on your own right now. Do you have a trash can in your room or bathroom? That can be your responsibility. If you share a bathroom, share responsibilities to keep it clean. Make a cleaning schedule and stick to it. Do you eat? You can load dishes in the dishwasher, empty it, and help wipe things down. See dust? Go ahead and get a cloth and wipe it down. Have friends coming over? Run the vacuum real quick. There's no reason why you can't learn and practice these skills now.

Your favorite cleaning friend will be the right tool for the job. Plenty of tools make cleaning simple and quick, and I encourage you to find the tool that you prefer and have it readily available. For example:

- If you've been mopping with a mop and bucket but notice that you never get to mopping because it's a hassle, try those spray mops you simply push around instead.

- If you have a dedicated dust cloth that you always go to, it'll take the guesswork out of what to use, and you can just grab it and go to work.

- If you have a toilet scrub brush in each bathroom, you can scrub the toilet whenever needed.

- You can keep a small scrub brush in the shower to do a mini scrub once a week and then a more extensive scrub once a month.

Consistency is key to keeping a clean environment. Finding ways to make that easy and, dare I say, fun will help you stay on top of it. Find time in your schedule for cleaning, and set a timer when you start. See how quickly you can get each job done, and next time, try to beat your record. Cleaning goes much faster and is simpler when you stay on top of it and don't let your area become super gross. Clean smarter, not harder.

Part 3: Next Level Skills: Setting Goals, Getting a Job, and Adulting Like a Pro

In this last part of the book, we'll talk about higher level skills like goal setting, creating a vision board and dream mapping, how to make a solid decision, what to expect when you get your first job, how to maintain a house, car, file taxes and how to become your own personal secretary. Phew! This is the final stretch and learning these skills will help you master your future and all the big adulting things. You've got this!

Chapter 13

Crafting Your Future

The things you do at this time in your life set the stage for the rest of your life. The decisions made during adolescence can have far-reaching consequences, shaping your personal and professional trajectory. Actively engaging in the process of crafting your future will empower you with a sense of agency and ownership over your life. That doesn't mean you have to have everything figured out just yet. But knowing how to have a growth mindset, make decisions, and plan and make goals for your future are skills worth learning. Nothing is ever set in stone, and failure will always be a part of the equation (it's the best way to learn!), but just because plans may change, that doesn't mean you shouldn't make a plan. By consciously thinking about and shaping your future, you'll enhance your present well-being and lay the groundwork for a future characterized by purpose, achievement, and personal fulfillment.

The Power of Decision Making

You make decisions about things all day, every day. What are you going to wear today, what are you going to eat, who are you going to sit next to at lunch, are you going to the game this weekend, and with whom? Sometimes, you have to make more significant decisions like which car to buy, which college to attend, and if it's worth getting a job or using that time to study harder. Knowing how to make a good decision is a skill that can help reduce anxiety and help you cultivate a sense of accomplishment and self-assurance. Not all decisions end up the way you plan, and that's okay. Every decision you make is a learning experience, but having the confidence to make a solid decision will help you as you navigate life.

Weighing Pros and Cons

Here's a classic decision-making strategy: weighing pros and cons. Think of it as a seesaw on the playground of decision-making. On one side, you've got the pros - the benefits or positive outcomes of a choice. On the other, you've got the cons - the drawbacks or potential downsides. Your task? To see which side weighs heavier.

When using this strategy, it's often helpful to actually write the pros and cons down, as opposed to just thinking them through, though that can also be helpful. Divide a sheet of paper in half and list the advantages and disadvantages of each option. Be honest with yourself. Don't overlook potential pitfalls because you're excited about a choice, and don't ignore possible benefits because you're nervous. This process provides a clear, objective view of each option and is a great practice when making a big decision.

Seeking Advice: When and From Whom

Sometimes it can feel awkward, but one of the best ways to make a decision is by seeking advice from friends and family that you trust. Just remember that not everyone's opinion may be the right one for your situation. Consider their expertise and experience. Do they have knowledge relevant to your decision? Have they been in a similar situation before? Also, reflect on their judgment and values. Do they make wise choices in their own life? Do their values align with yours? Take in each opinion, but remember that opinions may differ significantly, and ultimately, it's your decision to make.

Don't be afraid to seek advice from various sources - parents, teachers, coaches, or even professional counselors. They can provide different perspectives and insights, enriching your understanding of the decision.

Trust Your Gut

Trusting your intuition, or "gut," may be the most important strategy when making a decision. Now, this doesn't mean making impulsive decisions based on a whim. It means tuning into your intuition, your inner voice that echoes your values, desires, and experiences.

To tap into your gut feelings, find a quiet space and take a few deep breaths. Clear your mind and focus on the decision at hand. Consider opinions you've received from others and the results of your pros and cons list. As you sit quietly, observe the physical and emotional reactions that each option elicits. Do you feel a sense of calm or unease? Excitement or dread? These reactions can provide valuable clues about what's right for you. Trusting your gut is often underrated, but in my experience, it usually leads to the right decision.

Living with Your Decisions

Finally, let's discuss living with your decisions. Remember, no decision is set in stone. Own up to it if things don't work out as planned, but never forget that you can make a new decision. It's not about making the perfect choice every time but about learning, growing, and evolving with each decision you make.

Don't beat yourself up over mistakes. Yes, bad decisions can be jarring, but they also provide valuable lessons to help you make better decisions.

Setting SMART Goals

Goal setting is a skill that becomes increasingly important as you transition into adulthood. Whether planning on higher education, a career, or just working on personal development, setting and working towards goals is crucial for success in many aspects of your life.

Achieving your goals, no matter how small, contributes to a sense of accomplishment. Each success you have builds confidence and reinforces the belief that *you* can influence your outcomes. Goal setting also encourages self-reflection. As you set and pursue various goals, you'll learn more about yourself, your interests, strengths, and weaknesses.

While there isn't a right or wrong way to set goals, specific principles and practices can enhance the effectiveness of the goal-setting process. There's a simple acronym you can use for setting goals that can help you remember how to develop practical goals. It's called the SMART method for setting goals.

S.M.A.R.T. stands for Specific, Measurable, Achievable, Relevant, and Time-bound.

1. **Specific**. Goals should be specific and clearly defined. Vague or overly broad goals can be confusing and lead to a lack of direction. Instead of "I want to get better grades," try "I want to improve my math grade from

a B to an A."

2. **Measurable**. Goals should be measurable so they can be tracked and evaluated. Setting goals without measurable criteria can be challenging to determine success and can lead to frustration. How will you know you've achieved your goal? "I will know I've achieved my goal when I get an A on my final math exam."

3. **Achievable**. Goals should be challenging but achievable. Setting realistic goals ensures that they are motivating rather than discouraging. Establishing a goal that is too ambitious or impossible to attain can lead to feelings of failure and demotivation. Is your goal within your control? "I will study an extra hour each day and seek help when needed."

4. **Relevant**. Goals should reflect your values, aspirations, and overall life plan. This ensures that the effort put into achieving a goal is a meaningful use of time. Does this goal align with your broader objectives? "Improving my math grade will help me get into the engineering program I want."

5. **Time-bound**. Goals should have a timeframe for completion. This adds to a sense of urgency, helping you to stay focused and accountable. Failing to set a deadline or having unrealistic timelines can lead to procrastination and lack of progress. When do you want to achieve this goal? "I want to achieve this goal by the end of the semester."

It's important to be flexible and open to adjusting goals based on changing circumstances and new information. It's also important to balance setting short-term and long-term goals. Using the SMART method to set both short and long-term goals will increase the likelihood of success, which will give you a boost to succeed in more and more goals.

Let's practice setting one short-term and one long-term goal using the SMART method. There's space in the workbook to do this (page 109), or you can pull out your phone or paper. At the top, write down a goal you have. Write out one short-term goal and one long-term goal. Filling out the SMART framework will help you work out all the specifics, so just write down a simple goal. Once you have a goal written down, work through the letters (SMART) so you know exactly what you need to do to succeed at that goal.

I encourage you to take this a step further and revisit Chapter 8, Section 4, where you created your time block plan (page 85 in the workbook). Add your goal into your weekly time blocks so you know exactly what you have to do and when you will do it. Keep this plan somewhere you can see regularly - every day is great - so you are always reminded of what you're working on.

Dream Mapping and Vision Boards

Now, we're going to take goal setting to a new level. 'Dream mapping' and 'vision boards' are two creative tools used to visualize goals and aspirations, but they differ in their formats and approaches.

-**Dream mapping** is often a more structured and detailed approach. It involves creating a visual representation of your goals and aspirations in a systematic manner, often using a map or flowchart. Creating a dream map starts with a central goal. Then, you add branches or pathways reaching out from the center, representing smaller steps to achieving the bigger goal. It's a process of breaking down larger dreams into smaller, more actionable steps.

-A **vision board** is a collage of images, words, and symbols representing what you want to attract in your life. Creating a vision board is more free-form, where you just collect pictures or words and lay them out in an appealing way.

Both dream mapping and vision boards encourage you to reflect on your future aspirations and dream big. They help make your goals more tangible and visible, and they help to foster a positive mindset and belief that you really can attain your goals.

Dreaming big is a great exercise, but you must also make sure your big dreams are at least somewhat realistic. So before you get lost in the clouds of lofty goal dreamland, it's a good idea to always do a reality check. Balancing dreams with practicality means looking at your current situation, resources, and constraints and knowing what it will take to work beyond those. It's also about ensuring your dreams align with your values, capabilities, and the realities of the world around you. There's nothing wrong with dreaming big as long as you know what it will take to get you there.

So, take a moment to reflect. What are your strengths? What are your limitations? What are the potential obstacles in your path, and how can you overcome them? This isn't about dampening your dreams. It's about equipping yourself to pursue those dreams realistically and sustainably.

Now let's get to the fun part. The choice between creating a dream map or a vision board depends on personal preference and the preferred level of structure. You may find the detailed planning of dream mapping more effective, or you may resonate more with a vision board's visual and emotional appeal. You might even prefer combining both methods for a well-rounded approach to goal visualization and planning. If you're not sure, I suggest starting with the vision board. There's no right or wrong way to do it, but doing either exercise will help encourage long-term thinking and enhance those decision-making skills, and it will help to provide a roadmap you can follow to achieve your goals and aspirations.

You can use an app, note on your phone, some poster board, or there's a space in the workbook (page 113) to start a dream map or vision board. Next, I'll go into a little more detail on both methods so you can choose which one you'd like to try.

Vision Board

Vision boards emphasize the power of visualization. By regularly seeing images that represent your goals, you can be reminded of the goals you're working towards, and you may even be able to attract these things into your life. Vision boards often focus on the emotional and aesthetic aspects of goals (how they make you feel and what they look like to you). The visual elements are chosen based on the feelings they evoke rather than a strict logical plan, like dream mapping.

- Select Images and Words for Your Vision Board

If you still have magazines lying around, start by flipping through them or scroll through websites, hunting for *images* that align with your dreams. Maybe it's a picture of that sports car you hope to own, an image of a graduation cap to represent your academic goals, or a cozy home to represent your dream of owning a house someday. The key is choosing images that evoke a strong, positive emotional response that makes your dreams feel tangible.

Next, hunt for *words* that encapsulate your goals or their associated feelings. They could be powerful adjectives, motivational quotes, or even simple words that hold special meaning for you. These words will serve as a verbal affirmation of your aspirations, reinforcing them each time you look at your board.

- Arrange Your Vision Board

Now that you've gathered your images and words, it's time to put them all together to create your vision board. Think of it as painting a canvas, but instead of colors, you're using your images and words.

Start by placing the most critical goals in the center, the heart of your board. Then, arrange the other images and words around them. You could group them based on themes, timelines, or any other system that makes sense to you.

Remember, there's no right or wrong way to arrange your vision board. It's a reflection of your unique dreams, goals, and personal style. So, let your creativity flow and arrange your board in a way that inspires and motivates you.

Dream Mapping

Dream mapping places a strong emphasis on planning and strategy. It's much more in-depth than a vision board. Dream mapping encourages you to think deeply and critically about the steps, resources, and timelines required to reach a goal. This method often involves more details and specifics and is more suitable for those who prefer a more structured and organized approach to planning and attaining goals.

- Dream up a goal to map out

Start by allowing yourself to dream big. What do you want to achieve in the next five years? Ten years? Twenty years? Don't limit yourself. This is your future, your territory. You get to decide what goes on the map. Make a list of these big goals; eventually, you could create a separate map for each one. For this exercise, just pick one of those big goals (it could be the long-term goal you used to create a SMART goal) and write it in the center of your paper. Be as specific as you can with the information you have. For example, if your big goal is to become a doctor, don't just write down "become a doctor"; write down every detail you can think of about that goal, like "become a pediatric neurosurgeon working at the Mayo Clinic making $700,000 a year".

- Break Down the Goal

Next, break down this big dream into smaller, more achievable goals. These are the stepping stones that will lead you to your ultimate destination. If you need to, research what it takes to reach that goal. For example, suppose your goal is to graduate from Stanford. In that case, you probably need to know what you need to do to be accepted to Stanford in the first place, as well as Stanford's graduation requirements and what it will cost to attend Stanford, including potential scholarship opportunities. All this information will help shape the goals you need to accomplish during high school.

Take time to think through as many details as you can, but don't get too caught up in the tiny details that might just make you stressed out. This is supposed to be fun and encouraging, not something that will create stress and anxiety.

- Branching Out

Starting from the center, where you have your big goal, draw out branches to create smaller goals. Based on what your big goal is, you might have a financial branch, an academic branch, and an extracurricular branch. As much as possible, work backward in each branch with the steps you need to reach before you can reach your big goal. As you work out from the center, the goals will get closer to where you are right now. Take your time with this, and don't worry if it's not perfect. You can always add or delete steps as they come to you. Remember, nothing is set in stone. This is just to help you make a plan.

Update Your Vision Board or Dream Map Regularly

Just like your life, your vision board or dream map is not static. It's a dynamic entity that evolves with you. As you achieve your goals, your dreams grow, or you discover new aspirations, your vision board or dream map should reflect these changes.

Make it a point to review and update your board regularly, at least once a year. Remove images, words, or goals that no longer resonate with you and add new ones that align with your current goals and dreams.

This practice of updating your board not only keeps it relevant but also allows you to reflect on your growth and progress. It's a testament to where you're going and how far you've come.

Keep your board somewhere you'll see it often so you'll constantly be reminded of what you're working towards. As you look at the board, take a few moments to visualize your goals as if they're already achieved. Feel the joy, the pride, the satisfaction. This daily visualization practice can powerfully reinforce your goals and subconsciously prompt you to take actions that align with them.

Embrace Change: The Only Constant

If there's one thing in life that is constant, it's change. As you work towards crafting your future and setting and accomplishing goals, it's important to keep in mind that sometimes, despite our best efforts, life throws unexpected changes our way. Maybe your family moves while you're in the middle of high school, or an injury prevents you from hitting that P.R. in track. Having the ability to adapt to change is important, not only for our mental well-being but also for our continued progression.

We all go through different seasons in our lives, and it's important to recognize that each season has its place. This is called the cycle of change. You can think of it like the seasons of the year.

There's **Spring**, a time of growth and new beginnings. This is when you're exploring new opportunities, learning new skills, or starting new relationships. It's a time of excitement, hope, and potential.

Then comes **Summer**, a time of blossoming and flourishing. This is when you're reaping the rewards of your efforts, achieving your goals, and basking in the glow of success. It's a time of satisfaction, joy, and fulfillment.

But then, **Autumn** arrives, a time of change and transition. This is when you're facing challenges, making tough decisions, or dealing with loss. It's a time of uncertainty, discomfort, and introspection.

Finally, **Winter** sets in, a time of rest and reflection. This is when you're recalibrating, learning from your experiences, and preparing for the next cycle of change. It's a time of introspection, wisdom, and resilience.

Understanding this cycle of change can help you navigate life's ups and downs with grace and resilience. It reminds you that change is inevitable and also a vital part of growth and evolution. As you grow and progress, you'll recognize many cycles of change for various aspects of your life. Some cycles overlap: you may be experiencing Spring in one aspect of your life while simultaneously experiencing Autumn in another. Knowing this process can help you navigate these cycles as easily as possible.

Strategies for Adapting to Change

Knowing that change is part of life is one thing, but how do you actually manage it? First up, stay flexible. It's like being a tree that bends in the storm instead of breaking. When faced with change, adapt your plans, adjust your expectations, and be open to new possibilities.

Remember, rigidity is a recipe for stress and frustration, while flexibility paves the way for growth and resilience.

Next, as we discussed in Chapter 6, cultivate a positive attitude. Look for the silver lining in every cloud, the lessons in every challenge, the opportunities in every setback, and the potential in every change. A positive attitude not only makes the journey more enjoyable but also unlocks doors to new possibilities.

Finally, seek support. Reach out to friends, family, mentors, or even professional counselors when you're navigating a significant change. Sharing your experiences, gaining different perspectives, and receiving guidance can make the journey less daunting and more manageable.

The Growth Mindset

There are two types of mindsets: a **fixed** mindset and a **growth** mindset. Think about your muscles: the more you work them out, the stronger they become, right? If you have a fixed mindset regarding your muscles, it's like thinking there's a set strength you could reach, and you're incapable of getting any stronger than that set strength. Like you can lift 10 pounds, but you could never lift more than that.

What does having this kind of mindset do to your brain? You'd think that was just how strong you are, and there would never be any point in trying to lift anything heavier than 10 pounds. That's a *fixed* mindset. You'd avoid challenging activities because you'd think you can't improve or do any better than you are. You just are how you are.

Just like your muscles can grow and develop with the right kind of stimulation, your brain can grow, too. With a *growth* mindset, you believe that the more you do to challenge yourself, the stronger you become. So, when faced with a challenging problem or a new skill to learn, you might say, "This is a challenge, but the more I work on it, the stronger my brain will get!"

Having a growth mindset is like being a workout enthusiast for your brain. You understand that putting effort into learning, tackling challenges, and making mistakes is like doing reps at the mental gym – it's how you get smarter and more skilled over time. With a growth mindset, you approach new tasks enthusiastically, knowing that even if something seems difficult now, you can improve with effort and practice.

So, as you craft and work through your goals, celebrate your growth and milestones, no matter how small. Got through a tough day? Celebrate your resilience. Made a mistake? Celebrate the lesson. Embraced a new change? Celebrate your courage. Acknowledge your growth, appreciate your journey, and empower yourself to face future changes with confidence and optimism.

Chapter 14

The Path to Employment

Getting your first job can be daunting as well as exciting! Besides babysitting, my first job as a teenager was working in a candy shop in the local mall. It definitely wasn't a job that I wanted to make a career out of, but making my own money gave me a level of independence that isn't possible without an income. I learned and practiced many interpersonal and emotional skills, as well as how to mop big floors and do dishes in bulk.

Now that you've worked out some of your future goals, I would assume that many of them come with some sort of price tag attached. However, while money is definitely nice to have, getting a job isn't just about the cash that comes with it. There are several reasons why having a job as a teenager is well worth your time and effort. Employment provides an excellent platform to practice and develop essential life skills such as responsibility, teamwork, discipline, time management, and accountability. Working can also expose you to various environments that can help you identify areas of interest and allow you to explore potential career paths. You can get hands-on experience and prove to future employers that you're responsible and an employee worth hiring.

Landing Your First Job

Indeed, you always want to have your future goals in mind, and finding a job that will help you build skills and work well with your eventual career path is a great plan. However, for that first job, I recommend just going for whatever you can find. Your first job is a stepping stone; the value here lies in the all-around experience.

If all your friends work at the smoothie place down the street, that might be a great way to get in. If your dad knows someone looking for some help to file for a few hours a week, that sounds great. Don't be too picky with your first job, but don't take on a job that you know you'll absolutely hate and want to quit in a few weeks. Being a reliable, dedicated employee is a skill you'll want to prove you are capable of, and quitting a job two weeks after starting won't help you do that.

Your goal for that first job is to experience the application and interview process and prove to yourself and your employer that you are reliable and a hard worker. Always show up on time (10 minutes early is on time), be respectful, be teachable, work hard, and put in all your hours. Don't ask for too much time off; when you do, ask well in advance. Keep your phone away while at work and be an employee you can be proud of.

I recommend setting a time goal that you will commit to before you even land the job. Maybe you'll just work during the summer or until the end of the semester. Determine in advance how long you'll commit to working, and if, once you've started working, you decide it's not a job you're very keen about, stick it through until your goal time. This will help build perseverance and dedication and prove that you can make a commitment and stick to it. And since you put all your past job experience on future applications (or what's called a "resume"), it will show prospective employers that you don't job-hop.

In the sections ahead, we'll go over the basic process for getting your first job, which will also help you for all subsequent jobs.

Building a Resume and the Application Process

A resume is a document that summarizes your qualifications and experiences to potential employers. It showcases your skills, education, accomplishments, and previous jobs so employers can understand who you are and what you bring to the table. You should have a general resume prepared and ready at all times, however, when applying for a job, you should review your resume and tailor it specifically to the job you're applying for. You typically do not need a resume to land that very first job, but any employer will be impressed by a well-written resume. A resume will likely be required as you work your way into higher-level jobs. You can find resume forms and examples online.

To find out if a company is hiring, you can visit their website or a job search website. Alternatively, you could simply walk in and ask a manager if they're hiring and ask for an application. Some applications must be filled out online, but others still use a paper form you will fill out and return to a manager.

If you don't hear back about a job application within a week of submitting one, it's a good idea to reach out and ask about it. All you need to say is something like: "Hi! I turned in a job application last week and just want to make sure you got it." Reaching out this way shows the employer you're serious and unafraid to communicate. This one thing can often make the difference in getting the job or not. If you're serious about that job, keep reaching out every week until you get an interview or are told they're no longer interested.

The Job Interview

In order to be hired for a job, you have to go through an interview with your potential employer, who will ask you questions about who you are, why you want the job, and why you would be a good fit for the job. Always go into a job interview prepared. Preparation is more than just knowing the answers to common interview questions. It's about understanding the role you're applying for, researching the company, and aligning your skills and experiences with the job requirements. It's about rehearsing your responses but also being prepared for unexpected questions. Going through a practice interview with a parent or friend is a great way to prepare for the real thing.

Start by studying the job description. What skills and qualifications are they looking for? How do your experiences match these requirements? Next, research the company. What are their values, their culture, their vision? How can you contribute to their mission? Write down your findings and use them to tailor your responses. Know as much as you can about the job and company you're interviewing for so you can base your answers on that particular job.

Make a great first impression by going into a job interview dressed appropriately for the job at hand and looking and smelling clean. The very first thing an interviewer will notice is your appearance, so look nice and smile. Turn your phone off or silence it before heading into the interview.

A job interview is where the communication skills you learned in Part 1 of this book can really come into play and shine. Remember to communicate effectively. Speak clearly and confidently, listen actively, respond thoughtfully, and engage genuinely. Showcase your ideas and experiences while showing interest in what the interviewer says.

During the interview, be mindful of your speech. Avoid using slang or filler words like 'um' and 'like .'When the interviewer is speaking, focus on their words, body language, and tone. Respond to their statements with thoughtful comments or questions, showing that you're engaged and interested.

But remember, communication isn't just verbal. Your body language speaks volumes, too. Maintain eye contact to show confidence and interest. Use hand gestures to emphasize points, but avoid fidgeting or closed-off postures. Aim for a balance between professionalism and approachability, creating a positive impression.

To really leave a lasting impression, follow up several days after an interview by thanking the interviewer for their time. It's a small gesture, but it can make a big difference. It shows your appreciation for the opportunity and continued interest in the role. A simple email thanking the interviewer for their time can go a long way. You can also use this opportunity to reiterate your interest in the job and the value you can bring to the company. This reinforces your suitability for the role and keeps you fresh in the interviewer's mind.

You may have to undergo several job interviews until you are hired. Don't take a turned-down application as a failure. There are several reasons why companies choose not to employ various applicants, and you may never know the reasons behind not getting a particular job. You are entitled to ask the interviewer the reasons behind not getting a job, and this can be great feedback to learn from and use the next time you go through the interviewing process.

One last note for those of you that started feeling anxious just reading the above. If everything you just read about preparing for your first job sounds terrifying, I encourage you to do this: just go to the interview and be yourself. If you find yourself feeling frozen by the planning and preparation, there's nothing better than just diving in and experiencing it. Most interviewers will understand that as a teen looking for your first job, you're going to be nervous. That first interview will be the hardest, and each interview following will feel a little bit easier. Just like anything else, practice will help you. So even if all you do is go through several interviews simply for the experience, that alone is worth it. Keep trying! Eventually, you'll land a job and that will make you feel like a million bucks!

Explore Career Paths

Starting with your first job, each job you have will give you a clearer view of the path you might want to take for your future career. As you learn new skills and experience different jobs, you'll gradually determine what you love or hate to do. When figuring out what to study in college and your ultimate career path, use each job you've had as a learning experience.

For example, my son worked as a pest control technician in high school. This isn't a job he had an interest in doing long-term. Still, the experience taught him that he loves being outside and working independently. Even though he may never use his pest control skills in the future, he knows that he might be happiest in a job that allows him the freedom to be outside. That's a valuable lesson indeed!

Identifying your hobbies is also a great way to explore different career paths. Your hobbies and interests reflect what you enjoy and are naturally good at and what motivates you. So, don't dismiss them as mere pastimes. Explore them, dig deeper, and who knows, you might just stumble upon your dream career.

Think about all the school clubs and activities you've participated in. The debate team, the school play, the basketball team, or the art club. If you genuinely enjoyed it, it might be worth exploring further. Being part of the debate team could spark an interest in law, politics, or journalism. Participating in the school play could uncover a passion for acting, directing, or scriptwriting. Playing on the basketball team could lead to a career in sports, coaching, or sports nutrition. Even the art club could open up paths in graphic design, art therapy, or museum curation. Getting involved in different activities and clubs is a great way to explore various career fields.

What about hobbies outside of school? Those times you're doing something you love so much that you're fully invested, and time seems to stand still. It could be when you're strumming away on your guitar, lost in a book, or even out in nature, photographing wildlife. These are all great activities to explore deeper. Let's say you're a whiz at solving Rubik's cubes. You love the challenge, the problem-solving, and the satisfaction of seeing all the colors align. This could translate into a career in data analysis, where you'll solve complex problems and find data patterns. Or maybe you love to cook. You enjoy experimenting with flavors, creating new recipes, and seeing people enjoy your dishes. This could lead you to a career as a chef, nutritionist, or food blogger.

Here's the thing about interests - they're not set in stone. They can change, evolve, and grow, just like you. You might start high school with a love for science and dream of becoming a scientist, only to discover a passion for filmmaking in your senior year. And that's okay. It's all part of the journey. Embrace these shifts in interests. They're signs of growth, signs that you're learning more about yourself and the world around you. Don't be afraid to let go of old dreams and chase new ones.

Take just a few minutes now and list your hobbies and interests, including clubs and activities you've participated in. You can do this in the workbook (page 121) or on your phone. Add to this list whenever you think of new interests or join a new club. Put a star next to anything on the list that you absolutely love and feel a passion for. It's okay if nothing comes to mind right now - in that case, keep exploring! Once you have your starred activities, research what kinds of jobs you could do in this field. You never know where these ideas might lead!

Chapter 15

The DIY Guide to Master Adulting

We're nearing the end of the book now, but I want to share a few more things with you to make you aware of so you can truly own your future and master adulting. These are practical, next-level skills that will enable you to be a truly self-sufficient human. You can start practicing these skills at a very young age with the help of your parents or siblings so that by the time you leave the house, you know exactly what to do and how to do it. One of my favorite resources for some of the following skills is YouTube. You can watch and learn how to do so many of these things. Then, all you need to do is practice, and practice some more.

Home Maintenance

First up: Home maintenance. Specific skills are worth learning to maintain a well-cared-for home. One that doesn't look sketch. Taking pride in where you live, whether you rent or own, is a reflection of who you are. You can make anywhere that you live a peaceful, more welcoming home just by taking care of it. When looking for your own place, be sure to live somewhere you can properly care for, whether on your own or by hiring services. If that means renting an apartment with no yard because you don't have time to care for a yard, that's an important consideration, and perfectly okay. Below is a list of home maintenance skills you should know how to tackle before living independently. These go beyond keeping your living areas clean and tidy, like we've talked about earlier.

Tackle learning these skills one-by-one with the help of an adult or someone that knows how to do these things. You'll find this list on page 125 of the workbook so you can check off the skills as you learn them.

1. Changing a lightbulb. It is one of the most simple tasks, but you want to ensure you know how to do it safely, and know to use the correct lightbulb for the fixture.

2. Testing and changing batteries of smoke and CO_2 detectors. These can be life saving devices, and making sure they're always working properly is an important skill. Changing the battery regularly will not only keep them working, but will likely keep the device from waking you in the middle of the night with a battery warning beep that rattles your brain.

3. Fixing a clogged drain. Clogged drains are a common household problem, and knowing how to fix them can save you time and money. There are a few different methods for unclogging a drain, including using a plunger, a drain snake, or a chemical drain cleaner (which is the least preferred method if you talk to a plumber).

4. Replacing a toilet flapper. A toilet flapper is a small rubber valve that controls water flow into the toilet tank. If the flapper is worn or damaged, it can cause the toilet to continue to run or not flush properly. That's annoying. Replacing the flapper is relatively simple and can save money on your water bill and maybe your sanity as well.

5. Changing an air filter. Air filters in your furnace help trap dust, pollen, and other particles in your air. Changing them regularly is important to keep the air in your home clean, and doing this will help keep you healthier.

6. Cleaning gutters. Gutters help to channel rainwater away from your home. If they're clogged, they can overflow, potentially causing damage to your roof, siding, and foundation. Clean gutters at least in the Autumn after most leaves have dropped. Depending on where you live, you may also want to clean them in the Spring.

7. Mowing the lawn. I hope you were able to mow the lawn as a 10-year-old. It makes you feel so grown up and capable! Mowing the lawn regularly keeps your home looking tidy and well taken care of, keeps weeds from growing, and helps to keep your lawn healthy.

8. Watering the lawn. A dried-up, weed-filled, dead lawn is an eye sore, and trying to water a dried lawn usually just results in wasting water. Water your lawn regularly to stay green, but be conscious of your water usage and don't over-water.

9. Pruning trees and shrubs. Cutting back or pruning trees and shrubs helps keep them healthy and also prevents ugly overgrowth that could potentially cause damage to your property.

10. Painting. Knowing how to paint is a great skill to have. A fresh coat of paint can help refresh the look and feel of your home and will help keep

your walls and trim free from damage.

Basic Car Maintenance and Handling

Once upon a time, my brother-in-law drove his car several hundred miles with the "check engine" light on, thinking it was no big deal. In reality, it was a big deal! He had burned up all the oil in the car, which in turn burned up the engine, and his father had to drive hundreds of miles to pick him up since he was stranded in "the middle of nowhere." The car engine had to be replaced, which is not a cheap fix, and my brother-in-law learned a costly and vital life lesson. May that not happen to you. Here is a list of things you should know about car maintenance and handling from the moment you start driving a car.

1. How to check your tire pressure. Proper tire pressure is essential for safety and fuel efficiency. It's a good idea to check your tire pressure regularly, especially before long trips. Note that temperature extremes can change your tire pressure, and it's not unusual for tires to lose pressure when it's freezing outside. All cars, and sometimes the front vs. back tires on a vehicle, can have different pressure settings. Be sure to know what your car tire pressure needs to be set at before you start pumping air into it.

2. Know how to change a flat tire. Know where your spare tire is located and how to use a car jack. This is a great skill you can practice long before you have to use it in real life.

3. Check your oil level. Be sure to check your oil level regularly, again, especially before long trips.

4. Change your oil. Knowing how to change your oil is a great skill to learn and can help save you a lot of money, but if you don't know how to change your oil yourself, be prepared to pay to have your oil changed a couple times a year.

5. Check your coolant level. Coolant is a fluid that helps keep your engine from overheating. Check the level regularly and add more if it's low.

6. Check your windshield wiper fluid level. Keep your windshield wiper fluid tank filled, especially in the winter. Running out of fluid while driving during a snow melt can be potentially dangerous.

7. Check your lights. Ensure all your lights work properly, including headlights, taillights, brake lights, and turn signals. You should also check your high beams and fog lights. Do this once a month or so.

8. Speaking of lights, know how to use your high beams. Using your high beams is a good habit when other cars aren't around so you can see better at night, but be sure to turn them off as soon as you see another car's headlights coming towards you.

9. Check your wiper blades. Wiper blades are essential for keeping your windshield clean so you can see clearly while driving. Replace your wiper blades if they're cracked or torn or become brittle and are not cleaning your windshield properly.

10. Know how to jump-start a dead battery. Keep jumper cables in the car and practice using them *with supervision* so that if you ever need to jump a dead battery, you know how to do it.

11. Wash your car. Keeping your car clean is essential to protecting and maintaining the paint finish. You should also clean out and vacuum the inside of your car regularly.

12. Understand your car warning lights. If the "check engine" light is on, you should probably have the engine checked out. Wink.

There are many places you can take your car to that will do a general inspection and inform you of anything your car needs. But it's important to be careful and potentially get a second opinion if the list of needs or repairs seems long and expensive. You can avoid a lot of time, hassle, and spending too much money by knowing how to do many of these skills yourself. You'll find the above list on page 127 in the workbook, where you can check each skill off as you learn it.

Navigating Public Transportation

Bus, subway, tram or train! Whether you have your own car or not, live in a big or smaller city, you may have many opportunities to use public transportation. Using public transportation can be daunting, especially at first. However, planning ahead and knowing exactly what to expect can be an excellent way to save time and money. And if you have a valid student ID, some public transportation may be discounted or even free! There are opportunities to use public transit for shorter distances as well as for longer trips. Here are some key tips to know regarding using public transportation.

1. Get a student ID, and check for discounted or free fares.

2. Download the app. Most public transportation authorities have an app to help you plan your trip, track your bus or train, check fares, or even purchase tickets.

3. Plan your trip in advance. Before you head out, take some time to plan your trip. This includes figuring out which bus or train to take, where to get on and off, and how much it will cost. There are many apps and websites that can help you plan your trip, such as Google Maps, Transit, and Citymapper.

4. Be familiar with the fares and how tickets are purchased and used. Each city has its own fare system, so it's important to be familiar with how to pay for your ride. Some cities use paper tickets, while others use electronic cards or tokens. You can usually find information about fares and tickets on the website of the public transportation authority in your

city.

5. Be on time (on time is 10 minutes early). Public transportation is on a schedule and won't wait for you. You can avoid anxiety and panic if you plan to arrive at the station early.

6. Have your payment ready or have your ticket in hand. Don't wait until you're on the bus or train to figure out how you'll pay or find your ticket. Have your payment or ticket ready in advance so you avoid unnecessary anxiety and don't hold up the line.

7. Be aware of your surroundings. Public transportation is a great place to people-watch, but being aware of your surroundings is also important. Keep an eye on your belongings, and if someone seems suspicious or something doesn't feel right, be on high alert and find someone you might be able to trust and sit nearby.

8. Be respectful of other passengers. Public transportation is a shared space, so it's important to be respectful of others. This means things like keeping your voice down and avoiding playing music or videos out loud (use your earphones). Keep your belongings on your lap or at your feet, and avoid taking up more than one seat.

9. Likewise, be a considerate passenger. Make space for others, and be considerate of those with special needs or who are elderly. If there is a shortage of seats, consider giving yours up for someone who might have difficulty standing.

10. Ask for help if you need it. If you're lost or confused, don't be afraid to ask for help. There are usually staff members or other passengers who can help you find your way.

I encourage you to make a plan with a trusted adult and take a trip or two using public transportation. Take charge of the trip and practice the skills above. With time and practice, you'll feel more and more comfortable with public transportation.

Paying and Filing Taxes

We're not going to go into a whole lot of detail here, but there are some key things to know about the dreaded taxes. Taxes can be a confusing topic for anyone, but you're going to have to have some idea of what taxes are and how to deal with them by the time you're hired for your first job.

So, what are taxes? Taxes are a form of payment that the government collects to fund various public services, such as roads, schools, hospitals, and national defense. Taxes can be collected on income, property, sales, and other things, and are collected by the Federal government and individual states. Every time you buy something, you pay taxes on it. That's why if you're buying something that says $9.99 on the tag, you always have to pay more than that at the register. You must also pay taxes on any money you make at a job. Once a year, you can file for a tax return from the government, where they pay you back some or all of the taxes you've paid from your paycheck, depending on many variables.

When you are hired at your first job, you'll fill out a form called a W-4. This form will determine how much in Federal and State taxes you'll pay each paycheck. As you work, you'll get pay stubs, which are documents that show you how many hours you've worked during the pay period and how much in taxes has been withdrawn from your paycheck. So let's say you get a job making $10/hour, and you work 15 hours in one week. You would expect to be getting paid $150, right? But as you'll see on your paystub, you don't actually get paid $150 because you have to pay taxes on your earnings. I know, it feels harsh.

If you are considered self-employed, like you earned a bunch of money babysitting or mowing lawns, for instance, or if you have investments you've made money on, you'll need to fill out a form called a 1099. Since you work for yourself instead of an employer, you'll need to set aside your own money in case you need to pay taxes. Be sure to hang on to any receipts if you make your own money to prove where your money is coming from.

Once a year, you will file for a tax return and will need to use a form provided by your employer called a W-2. Your employer will mail this to you automatically at the beginning of the year. The deadline for filing tax returns for the previous year is usually April 15th. Until you're 19, it's very likely that you could get all the money you've paid in taxes returned to you, so filing for a tax return is worthwhile, even if you didn't make a ton of money over the year.

You should file for tax returns for both Federal and State. You can do so by filling out paper forms and mailing them in, or you can file electronically. For Federal taxes, you can file for free through the IRS website. For State taxes, you may have to pay a small fee to file, or there are websites and software you can use that could be free for both.

Personal Maintenance

This may be last, but it's certainly not least! The final task to truly master adulting is to be your own secretary and schedule regular health check-ups. This could include a physical, dental cleaning, eye exam, or any other routine screenings recommended for your age and health history. Ideally, you should see the doctor for a regular physical and get an eye exam yearly. Dental cleanings every six months is the recommendation. Luckily, most offices will schedule subsequent visits while you're there, so you only really need to remember to make that first appointment.

Making appointments can feel scary, but return to what you learned in Chapter 3 about making phone calls. Have your calendar and insurance information ready, write down what you want to say if that will help you feel less nervous, and have a paper and pen ready to take notes. Remember that the people on the other end of the phone are just people like you. They are there to help you. Ask any questions, and be sure to put the appointment in your calendar so you don't forget.

When it's time to go to the appointment, be on time (10 minutes early is on time), bring your insurance information, and be prepared with any questions you might have about that appointment.

When you start making your own appointments, you will truly feel like you're a master at adulting! You can practice doing this even at a young age while still living at home. Staying on top of your health is a lifelong commitment. It might not always be exciting or enjoyable, but it's a crucial part of your growing up journey. And it's worth it.

Conclusion

Wow! You made it to the end, and look how far you've come! We've covered everything from understanding yourself and your emotions to navigating relationships and high school drama. You've learned to communicate effectively, manage your time, and figure out how to be the boss of your personal finances. We've even tackled practical life skills like basic home and car maintenance, navigating public transport, and, yes, even filing taxes.

The power of life skills, as you've discovered, is immense. Each chapter, lesson, and exercise in this book has been a step toward becoming more confident, independent, and adept at adulting and owning your future. These skills are the tools you need to navigate the world, face challenges, and seize opportunities. They're the keys to building strong relationships, achieving your goals, and leading a fulfilling life.

But remember, this is just the beginning. The real adventure starts now, outside the pages of this book. It's time to put what you've learned into practice. Start small; maybe just help your mom with dinner a few times a week, or count your money so you know exactly how much you have. Then, as you gain confidence, take on bigger challenges. Try cooking a meal from scratch or budgeting for a month. Each task and challenge is an opportunity to learn, grow, and become a better version of yourself.

Ultimately, becoming a life skills champion is not about mastering every skill. It's about being willing to learn, having the courage to try, and the resilience to bounce back from failures. It's about embracing the journey towards adulting, with all its ups and downs, twists and turns, victories and setbacks.

So, here's my final note to you: Go forth and conquer the world. Be aware, be brave, be curious, and remember to have fun along the way. Laugh at yourself, learn from mistakes, try new things, and enjoy the journey. This is your life, your adventure. Make your story a story worth telling.

Pay It Forward

Dear Parent,

I hope you enjoyed reading and sharing "Life Skills for Teens" with your teen as much as I've enjoyed bringing this insightful guide to you. I truly hope you've had some valuable conversations and time spent with your teen as you've found time to read and learn together. Watching our children grow into adulthood is an exciting and nerve wracking time. When they fly the coop, you'll wonder if you've done enough and taught them everything they need to know. Being a parent is a tough job, no doubt! But I know you're doing great! How do I know? Because you've provided your teen with a book like this one. That shows you care.

Your thoughts and opinions are valuable to me, and I would love to hear about your experience with the book and workbook, if you also have that.

My mission is to make this book accessible to everyone. And, the only way for me to accomplish that mission is with the help of readers like you.

You see, most people do, in fact, judge a book by its cover (and its reviews). So here's my ask on behalf of a fellow parent and teen you've never met:

Please help by leaving this book a review.

If you've made it this far into the book, I ask that you take just another 45 seconds to scan the QR code below, which will take you directly to the review page for this book.

Your kindness will not only help another parent and teen, but it also helps me and my family, and I don't take that lightly. From the bottom of my heart, Thank You.

Simply scan the QR code below to leave your review on Amazon:

These companion workbooks and journals perfectly compliment the lessons taught within this book.

Find them on Amazon by scanning the QR codes:

Life Skills for Teens Companion Workbook

Kindness Matters: Journal for Teens

Gratitude Moments: Journal for Teens

Money Smart Teens: Budget Planning and Tracking Journal

(coming in 2024)

Mom's Go-To Recipes and Journal (coming in 2024)

References

1. Castillo, B. (2007). *Self Coaching 101*. Amazon. (https://www.amazon.com/Self-Coaching-101-Brooke-Castillo/dp/0977853993/ref=sr_1_5?crid=3VKS39U9LZJR2&keywords=self+coaching&qid=1698351669&s=books&sprefix=self+coachin%2Cstripbooks%2C228&sr=1-5)

2. Crone, E. A., & Dahl, R. E. (2012). The Development of Self and Identity in Adolescence. *Trends in Cognitive Sciences, 16*(7), 469–477. (https://www.ncbi.nlm.nih.gov/pmc/articles/PMC6667174/)

3. Stade, L. (n.d.). The 10 Emotional Skills Every Teen Needs To Be Taught. (https://lindastade.com/the-emotional-skills-every-teen-needs-to-be-taught/)

4. Grohol, J. M. (2022). Understanding What Your Emotions Are Trying to Tell You. *Psych Central.* (https://psychcentral.com/health/understanding-what-your-emotions-are-trying-to-tell-you#tips-to-i-d-emotions)

5. Hey Sigmund. (n.d.). Strengthening Your Teen's Social and Conversation Abilities. (https://www.heysigmund.com/strengthening-teens-social-conversation-abilities/)

6. Raising Children Network. (2022). Active listening with pre-teens and teenagers. (https://raisingchildren.net.au/pre-teens/communicating-relationships/communicating/active-listening)

7. Your Teen Magazine. (n.d.). Phone Etiquette Tips: 6 Must-Have Phone Skills for Teens. (https://yourteenmag.com/family-life/communication/phone-etiquette-tips)

8. American Psychiatric Association. (n.d.). The Mental Health Benefits of Simple Acts of Kindness. (https://www.psychiatry.org/news-room/apa-blogs/mental-health-benefits-simple-acts-of-kindness)

9. Greater Good Magazine. (n.d.). How Kindness Spreads in a Community. (https://greatergood.berkeley.edu/article/item/how_kindness_spreads_in_a_community)

10. TeenLife. (n.d.). 50 Community Service Ideas for Teen Volunteers. (https://www.teenlife.com/blog/50-community-service-ideas-teen-volunteers/)

11. Tottenham, N., & Galván, A. (2016). The Teenage Brain: The Stress Response and the Adolescent Brain. *Current Directions in Psychological Science, 25*(2), 130–135. (https://www.ncbi.nlm.nih.gov/pmc/articles/PMC4274618/)

12. Lester, L., Waters, S., & Cross, D. (2021). Stress management intervention to enhance adolescent mental health: A randomized controlled trial. *PLoS ONE, 16*(12), e0260842. (https://www.ncbi.nlm.nih.gov/pmc/articles/PMC8525873/)

13. Library of Congress. (n.d.). Life of Thomas Alva Edison. (https://www.loc.gov/collections/edison-company-motion-pictures-and-sound-recordings/articles-and-essays/biography/life-of-thomas-alva-edison/)

14. Biography. (n.d.). J.K. Rowling's Incredible Rags to Riches Story. (https://www.biography.com/authors-writers/jk-rowling-harry-potter-author-rags-to-riches-billionaire)

15. The Life Coach School. (n.d.). Self Coaching Model Guide. (https://thelifecoachschool.com/self-coaching-model-guide/)

16. Pasadena Bankruptcy Law. (n.d.). Bankruptcy Success Story: Walt Disney. (https://pasadenabankruptcylaw.com/bankruptcy-success-story-walt-disney/)

17. Child Mind Institute. (n.d.). Teens and Sleep: The Cost of Sleep Deprivation. (https://childmind.org/article/happens-teenagers-dont-get-enough-sleep/)

18. National Academies (n.d.). Nutrition in Middle Childhood and Adolescence. (https://www.ncbi.nlm.nih.gov/books/NBK525242/)

19. Academy of Nutrition and Dietetics (n.d.). Teen Nutrition for Fall Sports. (https://www.eatright.org/fitness/sports-and-athletic-performance/beginner-and-intermediate/teen-nutrition-for-fall-sports#:~:text=On%20average%2C%20active%20teenage%20boys,foods%20and%20heart%2Dhealthy%20fats.)

20. Eisenhower, D. (n.d.). The Eisenhower Matrix: Introduction & 3-Minute Video Tutorial. (https://www.eisenhower.me/eisenhower-matrix/)

21. Thriday (n.d.). Mastering the ABCDE Method for Efficient Task Management. (https://www.thriday.com.au/blog-posts/mastering-productivity-the-abcde-method-for-efficient-task-management)

22. Eastern Association for the Surgery of Trauma (n.d.). 8 Strategies for Achieving SMART Goals. (https://www.east.org/content/documents/8-strategies-for-achieving-smart-goals.pdf)

23. NPR (2023, April 25). Social Media and Teens' Mental Health. (https://www.npr.org/sections/health-shots/2023/04/25/1171773181/social-media-teens-mental-health)

24. Federal Trade Commission (n.d.). Children's Online Privacy Protection Act. (https://www.ftc.gov/legal-library/browse/statutes/childrens-online-privacy-protection-act)

25. Primack, B. A., Shensa, A., Sidani, J. E., Whaite, E. O., Lin, L. Y., Colditz, J. B., ... Miller, E. (2018). Social Media Use and Perceived Social Isolation Among

Young Adults in the U.S. *American Journal of Preventive Medicine, 53*(1), 1-8. (https://www.sciencedirect.com/science/article/abs/pii/S0747563218304667)

26. Consumer Financial Protection Bureau (n.d.). Teenagers and Saving. (https://www.consumerfinance.gov/consumer-tools/money-as-you-grow/teen-young-adult/explore-saving/)

27. News-Medical (n.d.). Investigating the Link between Cleaning and Mental Health. (https://www.news-medical.net/health/Investigating-the-Link-between-Cleaning-and-Mental-Health.aspx)

28. Veraki (n.d.). Creating the Ultimate Vision Board - Personal Growth. (https://www.veraki.com/blog/creating-the-ultimate-vision-board/)

29. Wikihow (n.d.). Help Your Teen Explore Possible Careers. ()

30. LiveCareer (n.d.). Teen Job Strategies. (https://www.livecareer.com/resources/interviews/prep/teen-job-strategies)

31. Family Handyman (n.d.). 100 Home Repairs You Don't Need to Call a Pro For. (https://www.familyhandyman.com/list/home-repairs-you-can-do-yourself/)

32. FIXD (n.d.). The Ultimate Guide to Car Maintenance for Beginners. (https://www.fixdapp.com/service/ultimate-guide-to-car-maintenance-beginners/)

33. Pennsylvania Department of Transportation (n.d.). Safety and Etiquette Tips. (https://www.penndot.pa.gov/TravelInPA/PublicTransitOptions/Pages/Safety-and-Etiquette-Tips.aspx)

34. Charles Schwab (n.d.). Does Your Teen Need to File a Tax Return? (https://www.schwab.com/learn/story/does-your-teen-need-to-file-tax-return)

35. TurboTax (n.d.). At What Income Does a Minor Have to File an Income Tax Return? (https://turbotax.intuit.com/tax-tips/family/at-what-income-does-a-minor-have-to-file-an-income-tax-return/L6HOdGp6i)

36. Internal Revenue Service (n.d.). IRS Free File Ideal for Young and First-Time Filers. (https://www.irs.gov/newsroom/irs-free-file-ideal-for-young-and-first-time-filers)

www.ingramcontent.com/pod-product-compliance
Lightning Source LLC
LaVergne TN
LVHW020928090426
835512LV00020B/3262